Editorial adviser/Harold Loukes

Frontiers of enquiry *the gods*

Written and compiled by ROBIN RICHARDSON

Director Bloxham Project
Research Unit Oxford

HART-DAVIS EDUCATIONAL

scandal

if his mother and his father had never come together
never never in all their lifetimes
never come together

then

SCANDALOUS SAYS EVERYMAN

in this town but not in that town, in this hour year
century but not in that hour year century, with this
mum mother mummy darling mutti maman but not
with that mum mother mummy darling mutti maman,
with this dad etc. but not with

SCANDALOUS SAYS EVERYMAN

'A way of telling who one is going to marry is by
hopping in and out of the squares on the pavement and
if one stands on a black line then one is going to marry
a negro, but if one should stand on a crack in the middle
of the square then one is going to marry a person of
one's own country. If one stands with one foot on each,
then one is going to marry a foreign person.'
Girl aged 14, Aberdeen

'If when you hear a cuckoo for the first time you turn
over the money in your pocket you will have money
all the year round.' **everywhere**

'If you are walking down a street before school starts,
and you see a white horse the horse brings you luck.'
Girl aged 13, Forfar

'I had warts about 5 months ago and I was told to cut
a hazel stick about half an inch thick, and cut as many
notches as you have warts. Then wrap the stick in
brown paper, tie with string, go for a bicycle ride and
drop it somewhere in the road. Do not tell anyone
about it. I have not told anyone till now. The person
who picks up the parcel will have the warts. About a
fortnight after my warts disappeared.' **Boy aged 13, north**

'If someone sees what is called a money-spider, he is
supposed to become rich in a short time, however if he
kills one of these spiders something terrible is supposed
to happen to him.' **Boy, Pontefract**

---

rain suckling but also regrettably drowning, and sun stepping up warmth but also regrettably dying daily, and fleshy
beasts coming but also going, and maize corn rice yams fruit ditto, and good health also ditto, and kids pushed and
pulled into the world or perhaps not, and a woman/man for loving or also perhaps not, and rich man poor man

beggar man

So: entering on magic,
       seeking wisdom from spirits,
       expecting secrets.
For: tired of talking,
       tired of intellect alone.
For: wanting to know what
       holds the world together,
       wanting to know what
       it's like deep down,
       wanting to know what
       keeps the whole thing going.

Goethe's Faust, Germany, eighteenth century

'If you see an ambulance you must touch wood or you will have bad luck. When the ambulance is out of sight you must keep your fingers crossed until you see a four-legged animal, and if there is more than one of you, you must have it the one who saw it first can uncross their fingers, and the others do not until they see other animals.' **Girl aged 10, Birmingham**

**Polynesian
corn god**

3

something to be done

Most of Priscilla's days were spent casting the horoscopes of horses, and she invested her money scientifically, as the Stars dictated. She betted on football too, and had a large notebook in which she registered the horoscopes of all the players in all the teams of the league. The process of balancing the horoscopes of two elevens one against the other was a very delicate and difficult one. A match between the Spurs and the Villa entailed a conflict in the heavens so vast and so complicated that it was not to be wondered at if she sometimes made a mistake about the outcome.

from 'Crome Yellow' by Aldous Huxley, England 1920s

"Of course, it takes time to get used to their belief in witchcraft, astrology and occultism."

DELHI INCANTATIONS TO AVERT DISASTER FROM PLANETS

From Our Own Correspondent

Delhi Feb 2

In corners of Delhi holy men are preparing with prayer and ritual to avert the disasters which they expect on earth this week-end from the conjunction of the astrologers' eight planets. One especially elaborate *yagna* (ritual) which was to have begun today was postponed, because, it is said, the stars were not propitious. Tomorrow some 250 priests are to begin incantations and ceremonies that will last for 21 days unless they are cut short by the feared cataclysm.

One has to look today for signs of apprehension, but it is real enough. Bazaars have been busier than usual with shoppers storing up provisions against the evil days ahead: some people are reported to have left Delhi for the countryside or holy places near by.

In Calcutta the defence forces have rejected many requests for the loan or hire of tents which the apprehensive proposed to to pitch in open places in case of earthquake.

The stock markets are showing one aspect of the apprehension; the ease with which a would-be traveller can obtain a seat on one of India's trunk air routes, usually crowded for days ahead, is another.

Some people may be taking comfort from the disagreement among the astrologers about what the conjunction will bring in its train. Those in Sikkim are saying that their country will be quite safe from whatever befalls, and one Tibetan astrologer has cheerily prophesied that as a result of the gathering of the planets "a diabolical war will be averted and notorious devils vanquished."

thief lady gipsy queen, and and and and I can hate my mother's guts if you want to know, and I can hate yours too my brother huh if you want to know though you probably don't and and and and I shall one hour finish dying

SOMEONE SHOULD DO SOMETHING ABOUT IT

and the point is they have, you and I we have. I painted my luck-love-hate on the cave-room wall, you danced your luck-love-hate before the altar, he and she read spiked netted framed caged hooked their luck-love-have in

red sky at night
dry stick scattered and wild geese flying
a wrinkled palm
magic available in various colours
ESPtarotouija
stars
and
gods

---

crystal-gazing 'the act of looking into a crystal, glass ball, or other *speculum*, or reflecting surface, with the object of inducing hallucinatory pictures. The pictures, of course, exist in the mind and not in the crystal.'

from 'Human Personality' by A E H Meyers, this century

On the left, a news item from 'The Times', 1962
The cutting on the right is from the 'Sunday Mirror', 1970

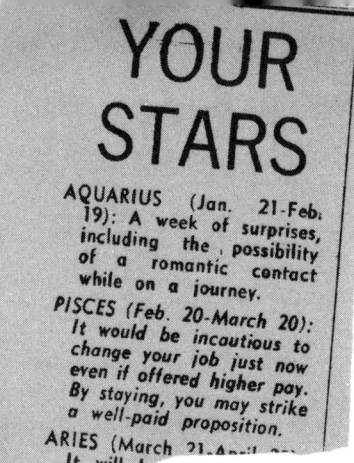

YOUR STARS

AQUARIUS (Jan. 21-Feb. 19): A week of surprises, including the possibility of a romantic contact while on a journey.
PISCES (Feb. 20-March 20): It would be incautious to change your job just now even if offered higher pay. By staying, you may strike a well-paid proposition.
ARIES (March 21-April ...
It will ...

The other day young Miss Y told me of Mrs X who always left her clock at twenty to eleven. Miss Y, feeling uneasy, had said: 'It's not right to leave a clock like that. Something is bound to happen.' Miss Y continued: 'And do you know, she died at exactly twenty to eleven.' [And] I was talking with an intelligent young engineer, who . . . told me quite seriously of a schoolmaster who had recently seen a green cross in the sky, of a doctor who had received a message on a ouija board from an Arabian suicide — in Arabic — and of an unhappy poltergeist stuck between the third and second dimension; as well as commenting on the curious way Aries males always went after Libra females. If our society is pervaded by beliefs of this type, then not merely is secularisation called in question, but Christianisation as well.

from a talk on BBC Radio, May 1966

Rumour ... (...t. 22): ... ing today, but tomorrow you will see through the whole thing. Devote yourself to the service of others, and you could reap advantages.
LIBRA (Sept. 23-Oct. 22): A sudden romantic attraction may provide the chief interest of the week for some Librans. Your routine may be upset.
SCORPIO (Oct. 23-Nov. 21) Frustrating influences may affect domestic life today. Opportunities for self-advancement may present themselves ...

no good or bad

It is not to discover what is going to 'happen' to us, it is not to forestall the blows of fate, that we should look to our horoscopes. A chart when properly read should enable one to understand the overall pattern of one's life. It should make a man more aware of the fact that his own life obeys the same rhythmical, cyclical laws as do other natural phenomena. It should prepare him to welcome change, constant change, and to understand that there is no good or bad, but always the two together in changing degrees, and that out of what is seemingly bad can come good, and vice versa.

Henry Miller, USA this century

There hath been a long time a foolish curiosity to judge by the stars of all things that should chance unto men: and thence to inquire and take counsel as touching those matters which are to be done. But we will by and by God willing declare that it is nothing but devilish superstition. Yea, and it hath been rejected by a common consent as pernicious to mankind. And yet at this day it hath got the upper hand in such sort that many which think themselves witty men, yea and have been so judged, are as it were bewitched therewith.

Jean Calvin, Switzerland sixteenth century

The fault, dear Brutus, is not in our stars,
But in ourselves . . . .

Julius Caesar by William Shakespeare, seventeenth century

She had said, 'We are lucky. We don't believe in God. So it's no use praying. If we did I could say beads, burn candles — oh, a hundred things. As it is, I can only keep my fingers crossed.'

from 'The Confidential Agent' by Graham Greene, set in England 1930s

News item from 'The Guardian', 1970

own would have cleared. Throughout the rest of the 1970s, the Church would face an increasing shortage of suitable men to appoint to vacant parishes. The total shortage was likely to reach 700 to 1,000 over the next 10 years.

The report forecasts that if the Church fails to fulfil its duties of spiritual care at a parish level, it would seem likely that such needs would be met by an even more rapid spread of practices like astrology and occultism, or they would manifest themselves in increased drug addiction and suicides.

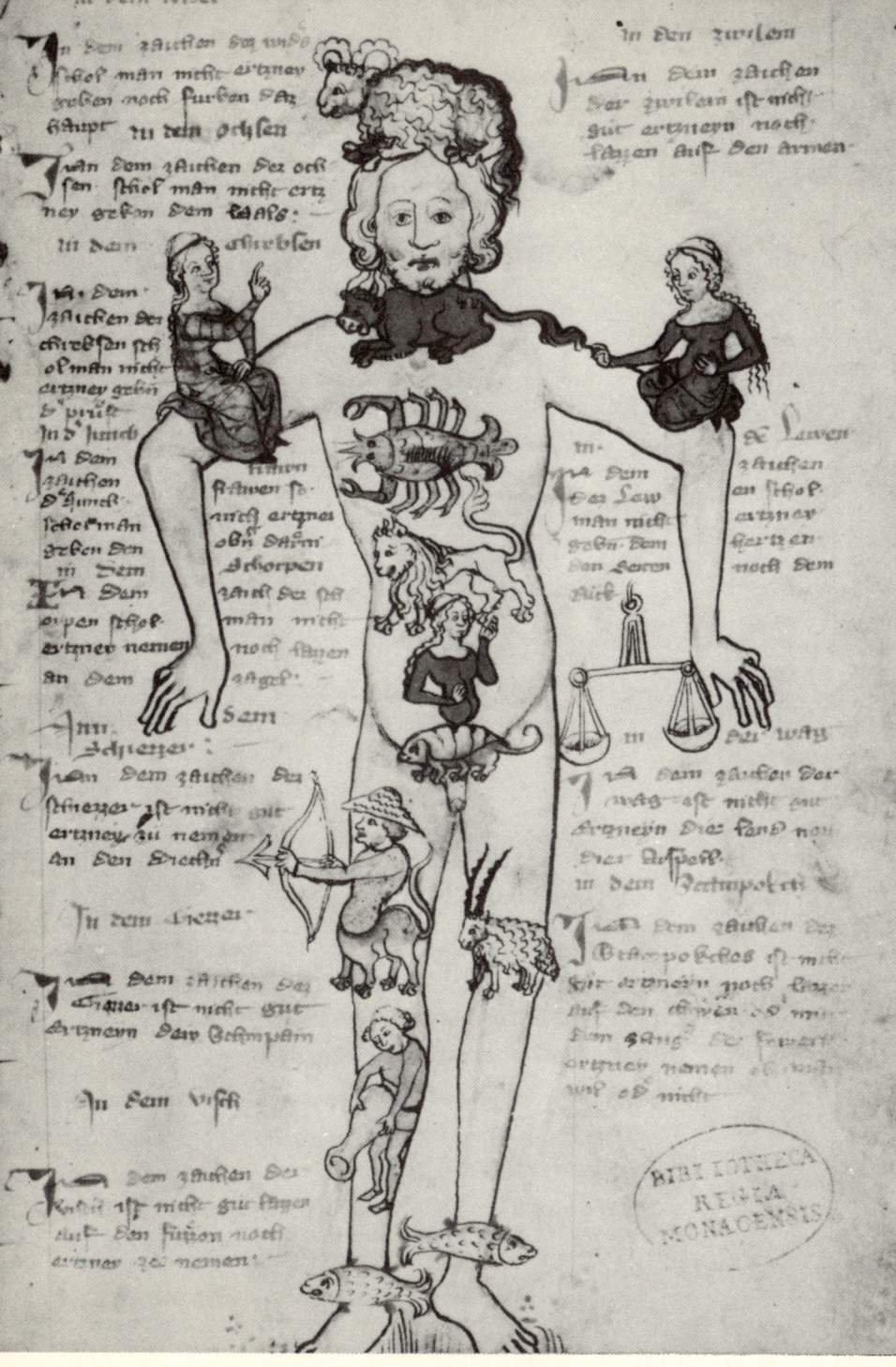

A picture in a book published in Germany, fourteenth century. The stars rule the body from head (Aries, the ram) to foot (Pisces, the fish). The text warns that medicines and ointments should not be used on parts of the body when the stars are in particular positions.

Below is an item from 'The People', 1970

IF TAUREANS and SCORPIONS have one thing in common it's that they are great protesters. Most of them strive to secure comforts, insist firmly on reasonable conditions for all enterprises and have a charming consideration for other folk's welfare. In contrast, LEO and AQUARIUS types respect authority and are always uneasy about large changes.

ARIAN and LIBRAN attitudes can vary from intense anger to complete indifference. Things must go well for them. It takes a lot to make them shout, however. When they do — wow! GEMINI and SAGITTARIUS people, utterly opposed to injustice, aren't averse to changes but reject anything that will lead to chaos.

CANCER and CAPRICORN folk dislike a fuss. They prefer subtle tactics to put things right — businesslike negotiations rather than a public outcry. VIRGOANS and PISCEANS are heated protesters about the woes of others but seldom complain about their o...

just luck

astrology
what do you know?

1 Astrology was based in the first instance on a study of the movements of seven heavenly bodies, believed to represent seven gods. (Incidentally, the seven days of the week were subsequently dedicated to these gods). Can you (i) name the seven heavenly bodies concerned, and the day of the week with which each is connected, (it will help to think of the French days of the week as well as the English) (ii) name the country in which astrology began, and (iii) give the approximate date?

2 To begin with, astrologers were concerned only with public events — harvests, war and peace, the welfare of the king. It was when astrology moved to another country that interest grew in individual horoscopes. Do you know, or can you guess, (i) which country this was, and (ii) roughly when?

3 Later, astrology was developed with reference to the 12 signs of the Zodiac. Can you (i) explain what the Zodiac is, (ii) name the group of countries where interest in it developed, and (iii) give approximate dates?

4 To work out a particular person's horoscope, there are two main things you need to know. What are they?

The answers are on page 11.

...h... ...audhry, ...hat's not his wife, ...e isn't a doctor. He used ...drive a bus for Glasgow ...orporation." Conciliation ensued.

● MUSIC to bring the roof down with. Bernard Herrmann, the film. composer/conductor, was recording Holst's "Planets" suite in the Kingsway Hall in London yesterday. While thundering through "Mars" the ceiling cracked and plaster fell from the heavens. Hasty conference of architects, surveyors and recording managers, and recording is allowed to continue—but with a general ban on the organ, timpani and "loud instruments." Touchy fellow, the god of war.

An English newspaper 1970

Do you

always	*score 5*	rarely	*score 2*
often	*score 4*	never	*score 1*
sometimes	*score 3*		

1 avoid the number 13?

2 say 'God bless you' when somebody sneezes?

3 Feel pleased if you find something you're wearing is the wrong way round?

4 feel pleased if a black cat crosses your path?

5 feel anxious on Friday the thirteenth?

6 cross your fingers if you want something good to happen?

7 touch wood to ward off the possibility of something bad happening?

8 make a point of not bringing white lilac into the house?

9 make a point of not walking under ladders?

10 make a point of not putting shoes on a table?

superstitions	low income → high income				
Per cent belief in particular superstitions by income groups					
believe in ghosts	23	17	15	16	16
heard or seen ghost (among believers only)	63	40	34	45	30
has lucky mascot	18	16	14	14	16
has lucky day	13	9	7	9	6
has lucky number	26	17	17	16	19
been to fortune teller	53	44	41	41	40
reads horoscopes regularly	51	45	42	41	29
thinks there is something in it	24	19	13	16	16

After Geoffrey Gorer, 'Exploring English Character' 1950

"It's no use worrying lad, if it's got your name on it there's nowt you can do . . ."

"Excuse please, how do you spell Simpson?"

What is your own score?

And what would be the score of:

your best friend?
your mother?
your father?
your grandmother?

Do you know the origins of
any of these customs and beliefs?

See page 10.

come to scare

Origins of superstitions (see page 8)

White lilac foretells death, it was believed, perhaps because of the association of death with 'drowsy-scented' flowers; crossed knives and shoes on the table were said to signify a quarrel, and the latter also death by hanging; people used to touch wood for good fortune because they believed certain trees — particularly oak, ash, hazel and apple — had protective powers; there were 13 in a witches coven — 12 witches and the devil; sneezes, whether for good or ill, were believed to be due to the sudden action of the supernatural; the most general significance of the cross, according to the Spanish authority J. E. Cirlot, is: "the conjuction of opposites — the positive (the vertical) with the negative (the horizontal), the superior with the inferior, life with death."

"It was just like you said it would be, mummy. The bogeyman came and got Charlie."

A Poltagiste

A poltagiste
Long and thin
I think one lives
In our dustbin.
When I go to empty the bin
He's gone.
He is scarey and frightening as can be
He's itching to touch things which are not his.
He likes to get me into trouble
By putting water into bottles
And opening new packets of soap
so that I get the blame.
He stands behind me.
Fighting against me
Staring at me.
He roars in the night
When the wind is soft
And all is dark.
He calls to his friends
To make me scared.
And then it happens.
The Ghosts.
They say I've come to scare you
I've come to scare you.
It echoes so much you scream and kick.
If I hide my head under the covers
He'll still be there
But if I fight him
He'll get tired
And die down.

Heather Ryan aged 8, England 1960s

Astrology — answers to the questions on page 8.

1 (i) sun (Sunday),
        moon (Monday),
        mars (Tuesday —
        French *mardi*),
        mercury (Wednesday —
        French *mercredi*),
        jupiter (Thursday — the
        Norse god Thor was the
        equivalent of the Roman
        Jupiter), venus (Friday —
        vendredi), and saturn
        (Saturday).
   (ii) Babylonia
  (iii) about 3000 BC.

2 (i) Greece, also Egypt — for
        there were many Greek
        astrologers at Alexandria.
   (ii) about 400 BC

3 (i) zone of the sky in which lie
        paths of sun, moon, and
        main planets; divided into
        twelve
   (ii) the Arab countries.
  (iii) from the seventh to the
         thirteenth century AD.

4 (i) you need to know the
        exact moment of his birth.
   (ii) you need to find out then
         exactly where each of
         the planets was just at that
         moment in relation to
         each of the twelve 'houses'
         or 'signs' of the Zodiac.

Fact (a dwarf man, or a giant cat) or fiction (a trick photograph)? A scene in the film 'The Incredible Shrinking Man', U.S.A., 1950s. If fiction, does the photograph nevertheless express something that is 'real'?

beginnings of the end

a tale from Melanasia: the skin

In the beginning men and women did not die. What happened was that when they grew old they cast off their skins like snakes, and then they were young and new again. One day an old woman went to a stream, as was the custom, to change her skin. She cast her skin into the water, and noticed that instead of floating right away, as usual, it happened to get caught against a stick. Then she went home.

She had left her child at home, and when the child saw her it screamed, and it could not or would not recognise her. 'My mother is old, you are young, you are not my mother, this woman is a stranger,' cried the child. In order to make her child calm again, the woman returned to the stream, where she retrieved her skin. She put it back on again. From that day men and women no longer cast their skins like snakes, and from that very day men and women began to die.

a tale from the Central Celebes: the stone and the banana

When the world first began, the earth and the sky were still close to one another. It was the custom of the Creator, who lived in the sky, to lower down gifts at the end of a rope. One day he lowered down a stone. 'What, a stone?' cried the first man and the first woman. 'No, no, we do not want a stone. Give us something else.' So the rope was raised, and it vanished into the sky. Then after a while it came low again. This time it bore a banana. The man and the woman took, and ate.

The Creator said, 'Because you have chosen the banana your life from now on will be like its life. When the banana tree has offspring the parent stem dies. So shall you also die, and your children will step into your place. If you had chosen the stone, your life would have been like its life, your life would have been changeless and unending.' The man and the woman grieved and wept over their fatal choice, but it was too late. That is how the eating of a banana brought death into the world.

a tale from Uganda: the dog and the people

One day God sent a messenger to men to tell them: 'You will never die. As the moon goes on for ever and ever, so will you go on for ever and ever.' The messenger was a dog. When the dog arrived with the men and the women, he said, 'I am a messenger from God.' But they laughed at him, and would not believe that he came from God. The dog became angry, and in his anger he changed the message which God had given him. 'The moon continues to live for ever and ever, but you will not live for ever if you do not give me food and drink,' he said. The people laughed all the more. The dog was furious, and he declared: 'From this day all men shall die. Only the moon will know rebirth.' And from that day, so it has been.

a tale from Togoland: the two messengers

One day man sent a dog to God. The message was: 'we wish to be reborn after our death.' The dog went off with the message. On the way he felt hungry, and went into a house where a man was boiling magical herbs. Meanwhile a frog also had left with a message for God. His message was: 'Men do not wish to be reborn after their death.' Nobody had told him to take this message.

As he watched the soup boiling the dog saw the frog go past. He thought, 'When I've had something to eat I can soon catch him up.' However, the frog arrived first and he gave his message to God. Soon the dog arrived. He gave his message. God said: 'Really this is very curious. I have received these two messages. As the frog arrived here first, it is his request that I shall grant.' And that is why men die, and never return to life.

All sorts of questions come to mind with stories such as these. Which do I prefer? Why, I wonder? In what ways, if any, do these stories please me? In what ways irritate me? Can I put my finger on it? If I were grieving over the death of a friend would any of these stories sort of comfort me, I wonder?

A twentieth century portrayal
of death: in the film 'Orphee',
directed by Jean Cocteau,
France, 1950s

is a man

One short sleep past, we wake eternally,
And death shall be no more; death, thou shalt die.

John Donne, England, seventeenth century

I wandered about the rubbish dump like this for quite
a time; I was very thirsty, and I drank from one of the
muddy puddles. If I got typhoid, all to the good, one
death was much the same as another.

J M G Le Clezio, France 1960s

A dog
that dies
and that knows
that it dies
like a dog
and that can say
that it knows
that it dies
like a dog
is a man

Erich Fried, Germany 1960s

14   **The picture was painted in Italy, sixteenth century**

a wonderful thing

'George, David is worried about death!'

He came to the doorway of the living-room, his shirt pocket bristling with pencils, holding in one hand a pint box of melting ice-cream and in the other the knife with which he was about to divide it into sections, their Sunday treat. 'Is the kid worried about death? Don't give it a thought, David. I'll be lucky if I live till tomorrow, and I'm not worried. If they'd taken a buckshot gun and shot me in the cradle I'd be better off. The *world*'d be better off. Hell, I think death is a wonderful thing. I look forward to it. Get the garbage out of the way. If I had the man here who invented death, I'd pin a medal on him.'

'Hush, George. You'll frighten the child worse than he is.'

This was not true; he never frightened David. There was no harm in his father, no harm at all.

from 'Pigeon Feathers' by John Updike, USA 1960s

and then what?

'It isn't clear,' he said obstinately. 'I want to be brave but first I have to know . . . Listen, they're going to take us into the courtyard. Good. They're going to stand up in front of us. How many?'

'I don't know. Five or eight. Not more.'

'All right. There'll be eight. Someone'll holler 'aim!' and I'll see eight rifles looking at me. I'll think how I'd like to get inside the wall, I'll push against it with my back . . . with every ounce of strength I have, but the wall will stay, like in a nightmare. I can imagine all that. If you only knew how well I can imagine it.'

'All right, all right!' I said, 'I can imagine it too.'

'It must hurt like hell. You know, they aim at the eyes and the mouth to disfigure you,' he added mechanically. 'I can feel the wounds already; I've had pains in my head and in my neck for the past hour. Not real pains. Worse. This is what I'm going to feel to-morrow morning. And then what?'

I well understood what he meant but I didn't want to act as if I did. I had pains too, pains in my body like a crowd of tiny scars. I couldn't get used to it. But I was like him, I attached no importance to it. 'After,' I said, 'you'll be pushing up daisies.'

from 'The Wall' by Jean-Paul Sartre, set in Spain 1930s

. . . . one hour finish dying, and this now is the last of a bunch of blind scandals, and in this same hour now the currents and strands of your life go snap, and your eyes explode, and they see where all this world you've been wending, weaving, flowing, turning, and is it all things new that is there, and was always there, just, just beneath the skin of your life, all things new . . . or is it finally the dark, only the dark . . . how or what, how and what, is the unknown.

the presence of the dead

Among many others, I interviewed Colonel Reginald Lester, Chairman of the Churches' Fellowship for Psychical and Spiritual Research, an author of impeccable honesty known to me for most of my life. I asked about the puerility of most spirit messages, which usually sound like Christmas cracker mottoes. 'Of course you do get triviality.' he replied, 'and I think that applies particularly to public meetings where a medium's message might apply equally to perhaps 20 or 30 people in the hall. They can all claim it and, in an audience of what I call our "message-hunters", most of them do.'

He spoke of one extraordinary seance where the physical medium was a Welsh bus driver: 'I went to one test session in Cardiff where we had all windows and doors sealed and everything, including the medium, was kept under very strict surveillance. During the three hours about 20 different figures materialised, walked around the room, and spoke. There was sufficient light to see the medium sitting in his chair, and the only other people in the room were our own group of researchers. These materialisations appeared to be fairly solid. You could not see through them, but there was this particular phenomenon: they formed gradually by a sort of vapour rising from the floor, and when they departed, they disappeared like a vapour back through the floor.'

'This was not mass hypnosis, was it?'

'It was not, because we had a very down-to-earth group of researchers there.'

'These 20 figures, did you touch them?'

'Yes, and they felt solid.'

'And warm?'

'That I don't know, as it was through robes.'

'How were they dressed?'

'Some in Chinese dress, some in Eastern robes.'

'And speaking English?'

'Speaking in English, yes. A remarkable experience, but I consider it an unpleasant type of phenomenon because physical mediumship is definitely at a lower level than the more spiritual level of mediumship which one should hope to attain.'

from a description by Alan Whicker of a programme he made for BBC Television, 1967

Dance of death: in 'The Seventh Seal', directed by Ingmar Bergman, Sweden, 1950s

... Not long ago I was called in to sort out an extremely nice set of young people ... One night at a friend's house they were persuaded to sit for kicks. Instead of fun they contacted what appeared to be a dead murderer, and his girl victim, and a suicide, each of whom gave evidential particulars (subsequently verified as more or less correct) of their fate over a century ago. It was a most terrifying experience, and they were quite unprepared for anything of this sort. They contacted their vicar for help, and he called me in. If this sort of 'rescue work' is to be done, and such apparently unhappy and still earthbound spirits (who seem often unaware that they have died) are to be helped, it needs hardheaded experienced people of good moral and spiritual balance to do it. Such spirits appear still to be hanging around their former earthly habitat, often full of unsatisfied physical desires (sex, drink, etc.) as well as harbouring tremendous desires for revenge against society, especially in the case of executed murderers — which is why I am totally against judicial hanging ...

Canon J Pearce Higgins, England 1960s

RECENTLY A WOMAN in South London has claimed that the great composers such as Bach, Beethoven and Mozart wish to communicate further pieces of music through her. Although she has no musical knowledge or background she claims to have taken down many pieces, including the 'finish' of Schubert's Unfinished Symphony, and many of these are shortly to be performed at the Wigmore Hall.

from an English newspaper, 1970

'... put on immortality'
In the first ten days after she died I felt her presence in the house three or four times. This could be misunderstood. It will be thought, by some people, to be only imagination but I must say what I have experienced. She was only a little girl, and although I was afraid, I said to myself: 'When did she ever wish harm to anyone — particularly her parents?' So although there was a sensation of coldness and fear, the age-old experience of men in the presence of the dead, our love for each other was stronger, and I knew that we should never forget and her separation from us was only for a time. It was perhaps as if she had come to see if we remembered, or as if uncertain as to where she should be, but however that was, we communicated in the language of love. Since then, although occasionally a photograph, her clothes, a letter, an old exercise book, her voice on the tape-recorder, or the thought of how delightful she would have been as a girl and a young woman causes us to feel sorrow, we have come to realize that in the long run all of life is only in time, and it is certain that the 'corruptible must put on incorruption, and this mortal must put on immortality.'

from an article by a man whose 8 year old daughter had been raped and murdered, England 1970

the bones were soft

witchcraft—
what do you know?

(answers on page 20)

1 Name as many things as you can that witches were, or are, popularly supposed to do.

2 All forms of witchcraft became punishable by death, as the result of a law issued in England in: 887? 1120? 1403? 1535? 1620?

3 The last execution for witchcraft in Great Britain was in 1575? 1650? 1722? 1800? 1861?

4 A coven was the name for:
   (i) a small group of 12 witches?
   (ii) a cat or owl owned by a witch?
   (iii) a wax image of an enemy?

5 A witches sabbath was
   (i) the action of spitting on the cross?
   (ii) a trial, usually held on a Sunday?
   (iii) an all-night meeting, held four times a year?

6 A familiar was the name for
   (i) the close friend of a witch?
   (ii) a witch's pet animal, for example a cat or a toad?
   (iii) a broomstick or other implement for aerial flight?

I live in Mazini kraal in the Gwaai Reserve. I am a witch, I bewitch people . . . After threshing and harvesting this year the accused came to see me at my kraal and she said, 'I gave birth on Monday night'. After that she indicated where she had hidden the child. I went with my sister Neiwa to the accused's kraal in the night when people were asleep. The accused came to call us. We went to the spot indicated by the accused. We found a dead baby. We cut the child in half at the waist. We left the lower portion of the body in the pit and covered it up again as we had found it. My sister and I took the upper portion of the child . . . On reaching my sister's kraal with the upper portion of the body we cooked it all and ate it. The bones were soft, we were able to chew them.

from evidence given at Tjolotjo,
Southern Rhodesia 1959

"Damned picnics!"

18

By her several Charms and Spels, she would convey man or woman 40 miles an hour in the Air. . . she could transform herself into any shape whatsoever viz

A Mastive Dog
A black Lyon
A white Bear
A Woolf
A Monkey
A Horse
A Bull
And a Calf

from evidence given against Anne Bodenham at Salisbury Assizes, 1652

Mrs Martins is an old witch, gentlemen, that's what she is, and she charmed me, and I got no sleep for her for three nights, and one night, at half past eleven o'clock, I got up because I could not sleep and went out, and found a walking-toad under a clod that had been dug up with a three-pronged fork. That is why I could not rest; she is a bad old woman; she put this toad there to charm me, and her daughter is just as bad, gentlemen. She went round this here walking-toad after she had buried it, and I could not rest by day or sleep by night till I found it.

from evidence given (by the defendant — he had assaulted Mrs Martins) at East Dereham Petty Sessions, 1879

With witchcraft, as with many other things in this book, there are three distinct kinds of question.

1 Is it factually true? If so, how would you set about proving it?
2 Or is it to be understood as picture-language? If so, what are the feelings about life which it is trying to express?
3 Either way, does it matter?

Diggory You're a witch, aren't you?

witch You mustn't say things like that, Diggory.

Diggory I'm not afraid of witches.

witch Of course you're not.

Diggory I eat witches for breakfast.

witch Every morning.

Diggory Any way, I don't believe in witches.

witch Of course not.

Diggory There are no such things as witches.

witch You're quite right.

Diggory Witches don't exist.

witch There are no such things as witches.

Diggory Witches aren't real.

witch There are no such things.

Diggory People just think they're real. I don't think they're real.

witch Some people say witches turn wine to vinegar.

Diggory That they blight rice and corn at midsummer.

witch That they kill the seedlings on the first of May.

Diggory That they shrivel flowers and shake fruit trees.

witch That they freeze men's legs and blunt farmers' razors.

Diggory Cause foals and lambs to be born dead.

witch Sweep the plague down children's throats.

Diggory It's none of it true.

witch Not a word of it.
(*pause*)

Diggory So my mother wants to see me?

witch Your mother.

from a children's play, 1960s

can it be proved?

Here are various things which some people believe:

1 'There is a monster in Loch Ness'

2 'Eating carrots helps you to see in the dark'

3 'Jesus Christ visited the earth in a spaceship on 19th January 1959.'

4 'Lennon and McCartney are the best songwriters since Schubert.'

5 'The world was made by God, and He loves His creatures.'

6 'Black people have lower intelligence than white people.'

7 'It is dangerous to walk within 50 yards of a pigeon.'

This list can be lengthened, of course, with other items taken from the pages of this book. Look at the items, and say of each:

a) Can it be *either* proved *or* disproved in such a way that thé vast majority of intelligent people would agree? If so, what kind of evidence would count one way or the other? What is the kind of experiment which could be mounted?

b) Even if it cannot be proved for certain, or disproved for certain, can you at least say 'probable' or 'improbable'? If so, on what grounds?

c) Even if it can be proved or disproved to *your* satisfaction, or even if *you* think it is probable or improbable, are there however other people who would remain unconvinced? If so, what kind of people?

d) But whether it can be proved or not, or whether people are convinced or not, does it *matter*? Does it matter what people believe? If so, on what grounds does it matter? (The questions here include also: what would people *do* who believed this? Would it *matter* if they did? Would it do any harm — to themselves or to others? Would it do any good?)

(By the way: do you agree that of the items above: one can be proved to be correct, two can be proved to be incorrect, one is extremely improbable, one *can* be proved or disproved though scientists are not yet sure one way or the other, and two can be neither proved nor disproved).

telepathy

Here are four of mankind's most basic pictures. With a friend, you may care to try using them in a telepathy experiment. Fix one in your mind's eye, and then try to transmit it. See how often you — and your friend — can get it right.

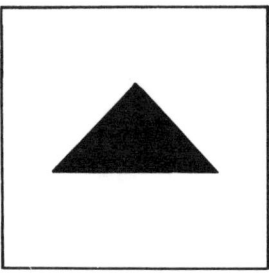

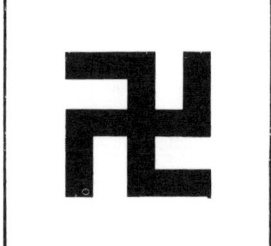

Witchcraft — answers to the questions on page 18.

1 aerial flight, abuse of sacred things including spitting on the cross, homage and prayer to the devil, sexual intercourse with the devil or with spirits (succubi and incubi), killing and eating children, orgies, 'sabbaths', dismembering corpses, making love-potions, causing disease to people, animals and crops . . . .

2 1403

3 1722

4 a group of witches

5 an all-night meeting

6 a pet

on a day in November 1963 author and journalist **Beverley Nichols** was giving an unscripted broadcast for the Canadian Broadcasting Company. The theme was the British monarchy. In his mind's eye he had summoned up a picture of the Queen driving down the Mall:

The mental picture was exceptionally vivid; I seemed to see the sunlight sparkling on the polished breastplates and hear the clatter of the horses' hooves . . . that most evocative of all the sounds of London.

Then, without any warning, I had a sharp feeling of discomfort, almost of nausea, accompanied by an acute headache. The picture of the Queen and her cavalcade vanished as swiftly as if it had been blacked out in a theatrical performance, to be replaced by an equally vivid picture of President Kennedy driving in an open car, flanked by his escort of motor-bicyclists with their snarling exhausts. And, as though it were being dictated to me, I began to describe this scene.

All this is on the tape . . .

The interviewer held up his hand and flicked his fingers. He switched off the recorder.

'O.K. That was swell. Fifteen minutes to the dot.'

I felt rather pleased with myself. Evidently he hadn't noticed the emotional tension of the last few minutes. I said: 'Wasn't the ending a bit abrupt?'

'Sure. But that's how we like it.' He pressed a button and the tape spun back. 'Let's play back the last part. Your switch to Kennedy took me off my guard. But it was a good curtain.' . . .

. . . 'And now I think we've earned a drink.'

He walked to the door and opened it. I followed him. As we stepped outside we heard the sound of footsteps running. A little man with a white face turned the corner. He came to a halt in front of us. He stared at us, not quite seeing us.

'President Kennedy,' he blurted out, 'has been assassinated. Six minutes ago.'

from 'Powers That Be' by Beverley Nichols 1966

the sixth sense

The nearest parallel in nature is the way that flocks of birds fly in formation. Their movements are too uniform to be accounted for by some form of call signal listened to by the alert minds of the flock, and then translated by each individual bird into the appropriate action; it seems as if the instructions are passed direct to their flight control mechanism — on the analogy of a blind landing system for aircraft, where the controller's landing instructions are transmitted direct to an automatic pilot. Human beings, it is thought, once had a sixth sense, but allowed it to fall into disuse, possibly because the development of speech enabled instructions to be given direct without it. A few people retain the faculty to some degree (or perhaps many people retain it, but only a few learn how to exploit it).

from 'Fringe Medicine' by Brian Inglis, England 1960s

"They don't cast spells like they used to."

getting the right word

Here are some dictionary definitions of ten words: delusion, faith, legend, magic, myth, poetry, religion, superstition, symbol, truth. Can you match each definition to its word?

1 A purely fictitious narrative usually involving supernatural persons, actions or events, and embodying some popular idea concerning natural or historical phenomena.

2 The pretended art of influencing the course of events, and of producing marvellous physical phenomena, by processes supposed to impel the intervention of spiritual beings.

3 An unauthentic or non-historical story, especially one handed down by tradition from early times and popularly regarded as historical.

4 Unreasoning awe or fear of something unknown, mysterious or imaginary; belief or practice founded on fear or ignorance.

5 Something that stands for, represents, or denotes something else; (not by exact resemblance, but by vague suggestion, or by some accidental or conventional relation) especially a material object representing or taken to represent something immaterial or abstract, as a being, idea, or condition.

6 Recognition on the part of man of some higher unseen power as having control of his destiny, and as being entitled to obedience, reverence, and worship; the general mental and moral attitude resulting from this belief, with reference to its effect upon the individual or the community.

7 Confidence, reliance, trust (in the ability, goodness, etc. of a person; in the worth of a thing; or in the truth of a statement or doctrine). In early use, only with reference to religious objects; this is still the prevalent application, and often colours the wider use.

8 The fact or facts; the actual state of the case; the matter or circumstance as it really is.

9 Anything that deceives the mind with a false impression; a deception; a fixed false opinion or belief with regard to objective things, especially as a form of mental derangement.

10 The expression or embodiment of thought, imagination, or feeling, in language adapted to stir the imagination and emotions.

The questions then, of course, are: can you find things in this book which illustrate each of the above definitions? And which are the things in this book to which, from differing viewpoints, several of these definitions could be applied at once?

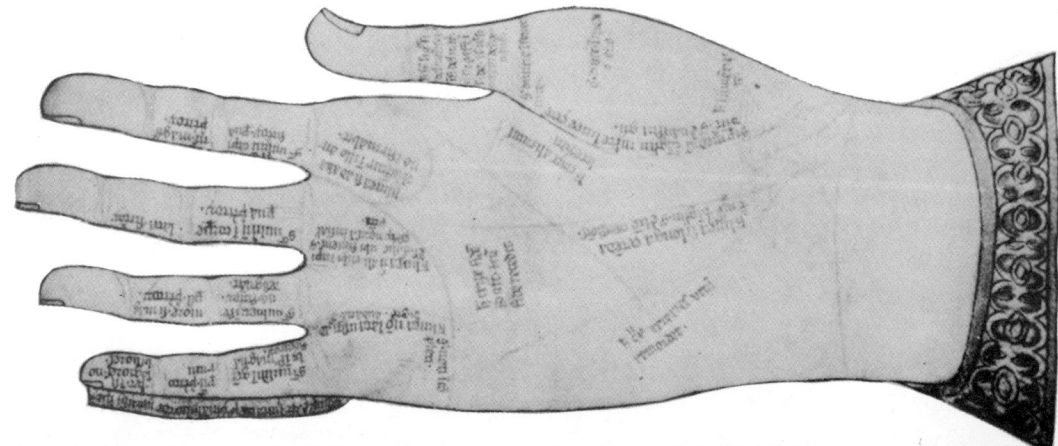

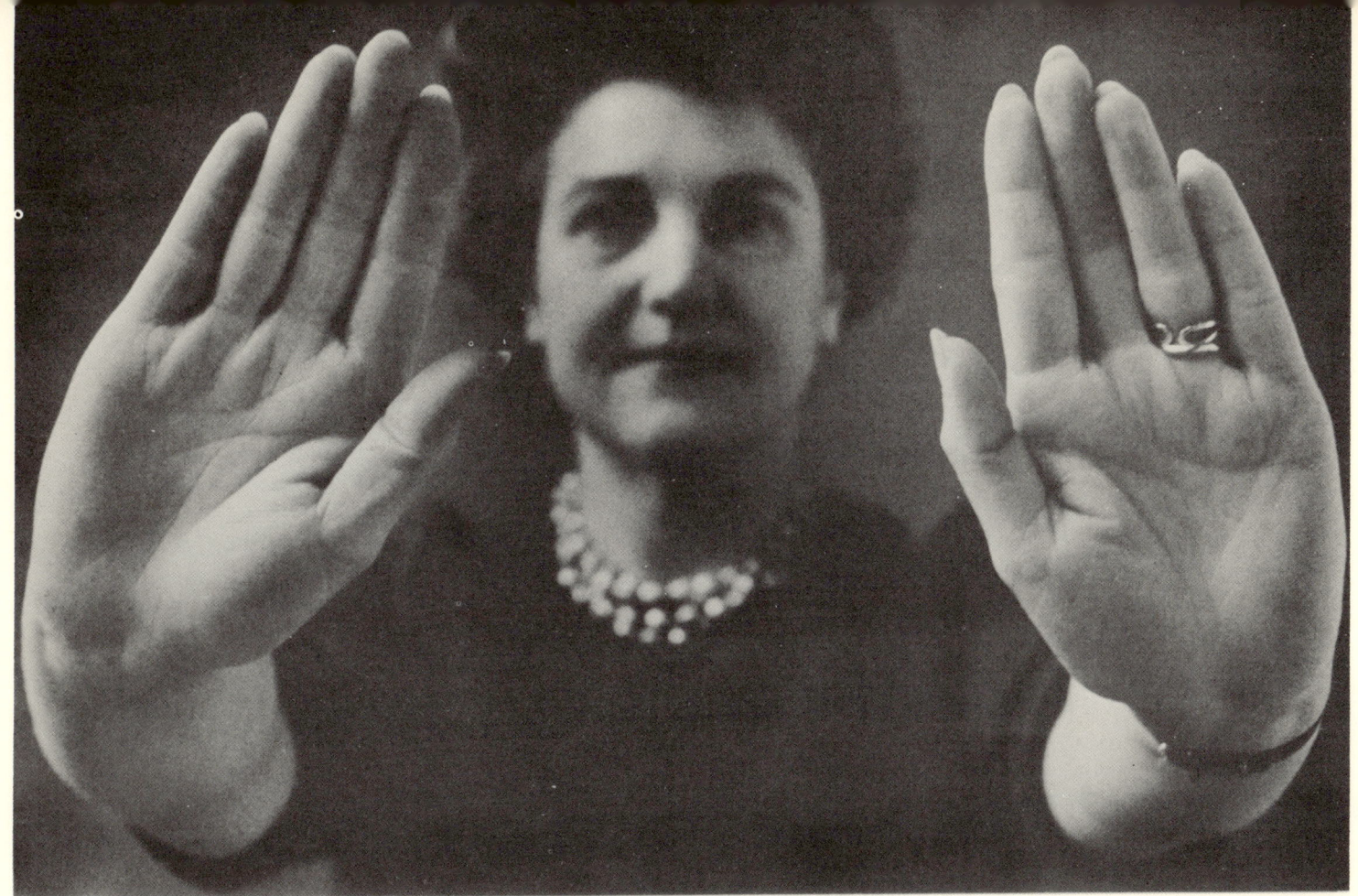

The picture on the left is from a 13th century manuscript. The lines from the wrist towards the fingers are the 'lifeline' (by the thumb), the 'fateline' (in the centre), and the 'line of intuition'. The other two lines are the 'heartline' (nearer the fingers) and the 'headline'.

Right: from an article by Jo Sheridan in 'Woman', 1970.

and material ambitions. A cross under the **Mount of Mercury** shows that you are mentally in affinity with the psychic scene. You enjoy going to fortune-tellers, attending séances, reading ghost stories or books about occult subjects.

Other indications of intuition and psychic powers you may find in your hand are: a **Heartline** which completely encircles the Mount of Mercury; a **Headline** which slopes downwards to the Mount of the Moon; a Triangle on the Mount of Saturn; the figure 8 formed by two Islands at the base of the Fateline; the **Line of Intuition** which appears as a semi-circle, beginning in the Mount of Mercury and ending low on the Mount of the Moon —if your hand shows *this* line, you are sensitive and highly perceptive, with a great intuitive power—the occult will appeal to you and you may even possess special psychic gifts.

23

civilising the world

Here are pictures, and descriptions, of three gods or goddesses. Can you match each picture to a description? The names of these three are ISIS, SIVA, and DOMOVOI. Which is which, do you think, or do you happen to know? The countries of origin are Central Europe, Egypt and India — which god belongs where?

(answers on page 34)

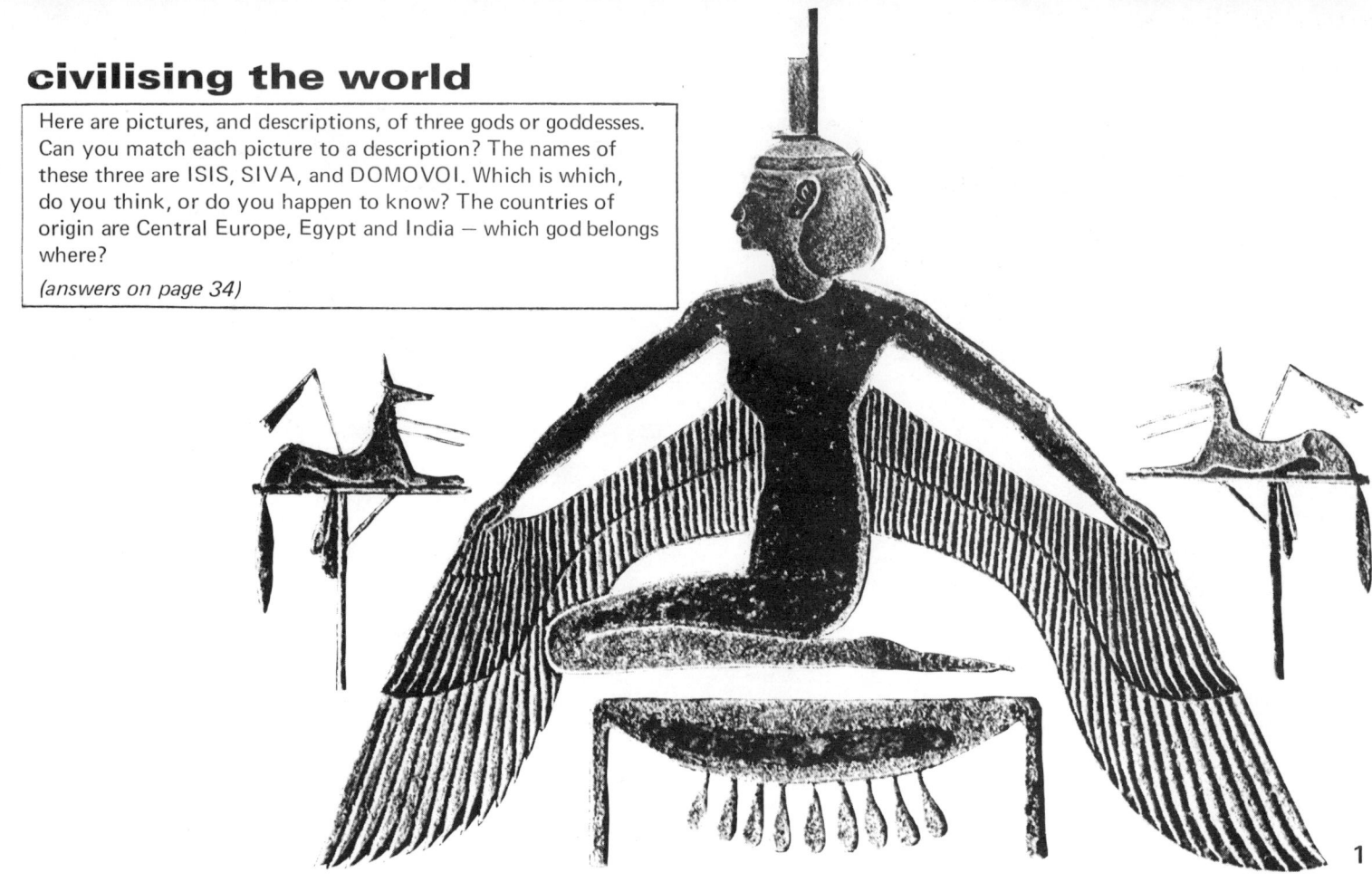

1

a) He wore snakes at his throat, at his waist, at his four wrists, he was power. He could: destroy as time destroys to ashes and dust. He could: tear the skin from a tiger with the nail of his little finger. He could also: spurt life into the world, could push life through the limbs of men and women. He could: dance. In his dances joined throbbing makers and breakers together, in his dances joined warmth and corpses together, in his dances every man and every woman, and every grain and every virus, joined captured together. His dances set free.

b) Sometimes disguised he was as a pet around the house, disguised sometimes he was a bundle of hay. Seldom he was seen, but frequently he was heard, his voice groaning, sobbing, or else whispering, caressing. His closest relations lived in yards, sheds, barns, in the forest, in fields, in the mill-pond, were tear-aways, but himself he preferred the

24

2

3

houses of men and women. He would dwell tame kindly beneath the front door. At night he would emerge for crumbs, and sometimes in the day he would (it was the sort of thing he did) pull a woman's hair: to warn her thus that her husband was going to beat her.

c) Warm wife womanly of the wisest and best of the gods, he her husband with his handsome height brought wine, ploughs also he brought in and grain, also music in and peace, and he stamped out cannibals, while she his helpmate taught grinding, baking, spinning, weaving, also seeking, healing, tending, taught married life and children too, oh she and her husband between them civilised the world, he like the river pushing into her, and she like the rich plains waiting, and teeming, and caring.

25

held high

4

Here are pictures and descriptions of three more gods.
Again can you match each picture to a description?
The names and countries of origin are:
TEZCATLICOPA, APHRODITE, ODIN;
Greece, Northern Europe, Mexico.
Can you match them all up?

(answers on page 35)

d) love she made not war with the gleaming of her hair with the silver of her feet with the smiling of her lips with the calm on her fingers with every speck of her presence she invited aroused summoned compelled shaggy wolves frisked for her bristling lions sat up for her there was nothing men and women would not do for her for her fathers lost daughters as if slaughtered mothers their sons as if drowned for her sometimes husbands and wives were ripped from each other for what she could do was change stone into flesh for what she did was change stone into warm limbs for loving.

e) Fierce his face as the sun which blinds, beats, melts, shrivels, but without which nothing, neither fruit of tree nor fruit of man, ripens. In the dark, he prowled as a jaguar, or as a head-in-hand monster. But primarily his desires were of, as his nature was of, the sunlight, and what in the sunlight he most desired was that one of the handsomest of his

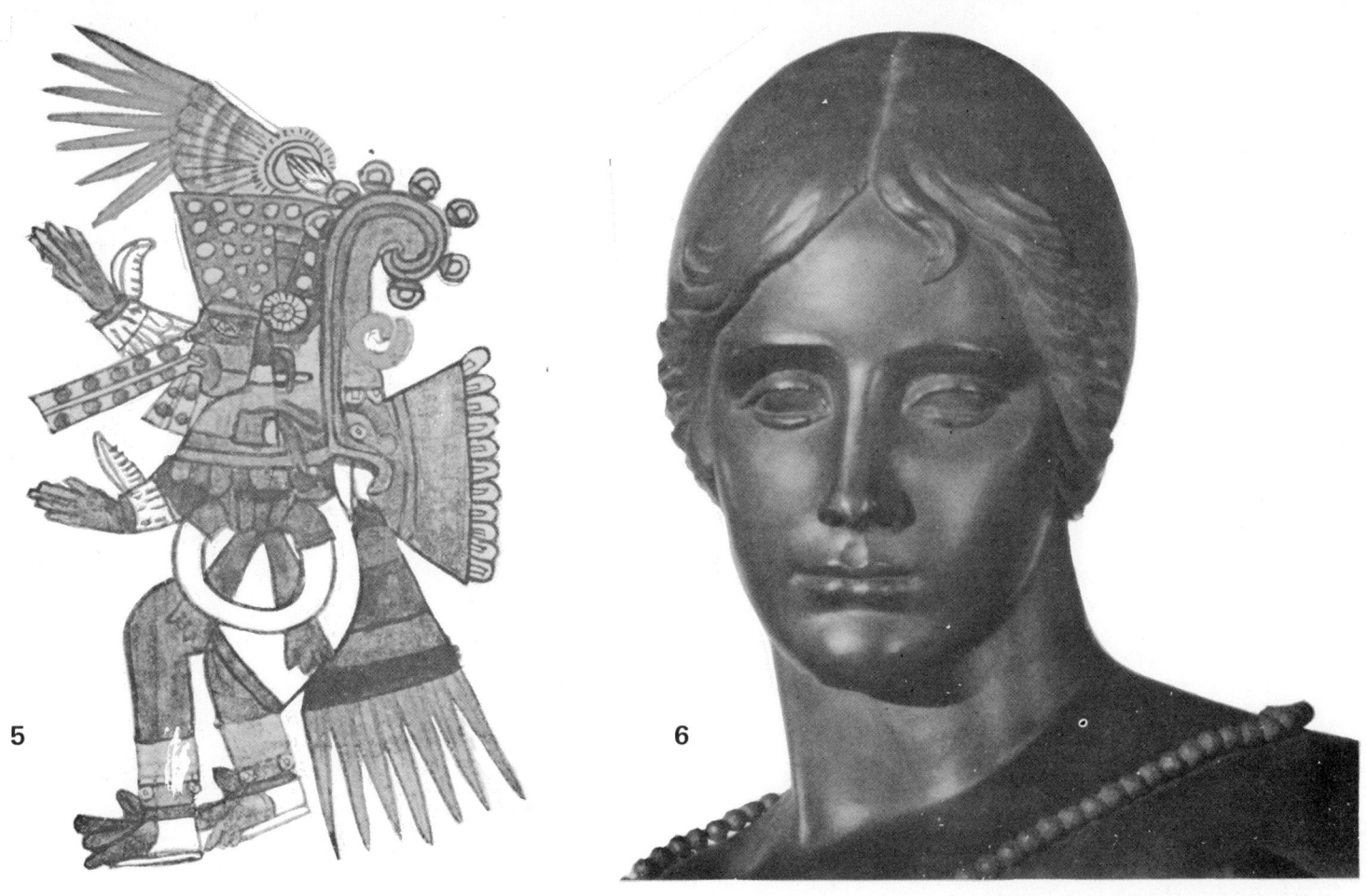

5   6

followers should: robe richly, play flute, smoke, have four wives, live thus for a year from midsummer to midsummer, come then at the end to a place on the mountain, where with a single scoop of the knife his chest was jagged open, and his heart ripped out, and his heart held high, wriggling yet and steaming, that the world might continue to ripen.

f) In a hall with 540 doors he dwelt, each door wide for 800 warriors marching abreast. The walls of it were hung with shields, with breastplates and swords, and his companions there were wolves and bears of men, they were the bravest of all battle fallen. When he visited the world: it was on his eight hooved horse hunting berserk in the wind and the sky, or as a fish or a bull, a bird or a snake, as a monster, a bear, as a poet also, frequently it was on the battlefield, and once, to drive fresh blood through his own veins, and through the veins of men, he hung for nine days and nights from a windswept ash tree, dying.

fact or fiction chart

You see, read or hear a story. It may be: an opera, a film a newspaper headline, a joke, a painting, a High Mass, a novel, etc etc etc. This chart shows the channels which your mind moves along when you hear the story. Of course, you don't usually move *consciously,* and often you move through it so fast or so absorbed that obviously you couldn't possibly stop to think and look at the way you're going. It probably wouldn't be a very good story if you had to keep wondering about it. However, take some of the stories in this book, and plot your way through the chart with them.

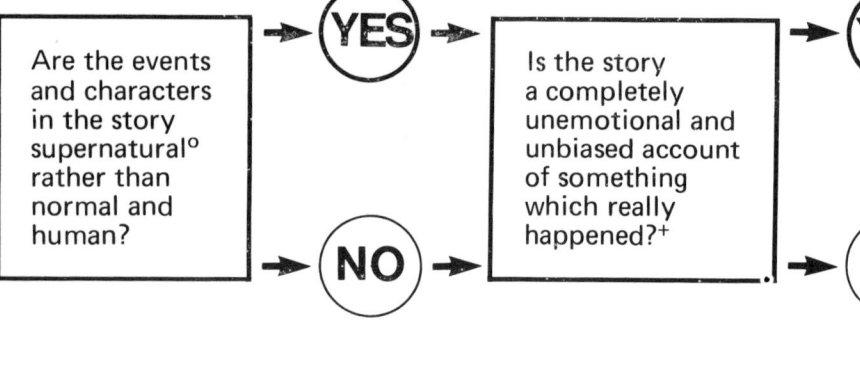

°*Dictionary definition of supernatural:*
'due to or manifesting some agency
above the forces of nature,
outside the ordinary operation
of cause and effect'.

+*See quotation from Claud Cockburn, page 33.*

* *See pages 30/31.*

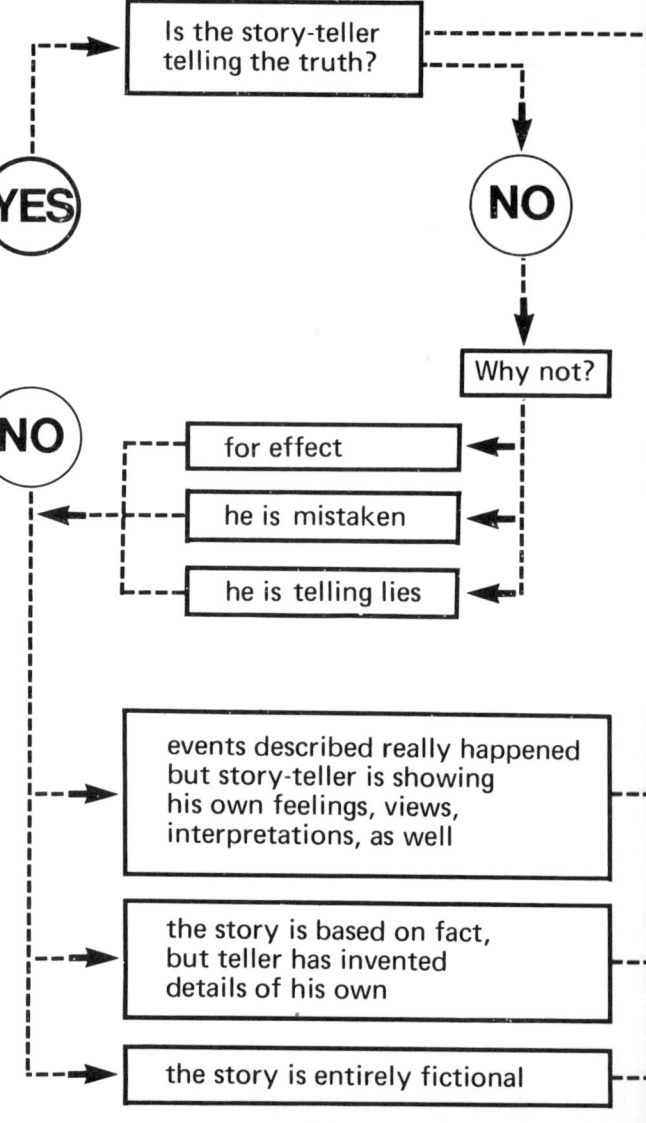

Is the story-teller telling the truth?

NO

Why not?

for effect

he is mistaken

he is telling lies

events described really happened but story-teller is showing his own feelings, views, interpretations, as well

the story is based on fact, but teller has invented details of his own

the story is entirely fictional

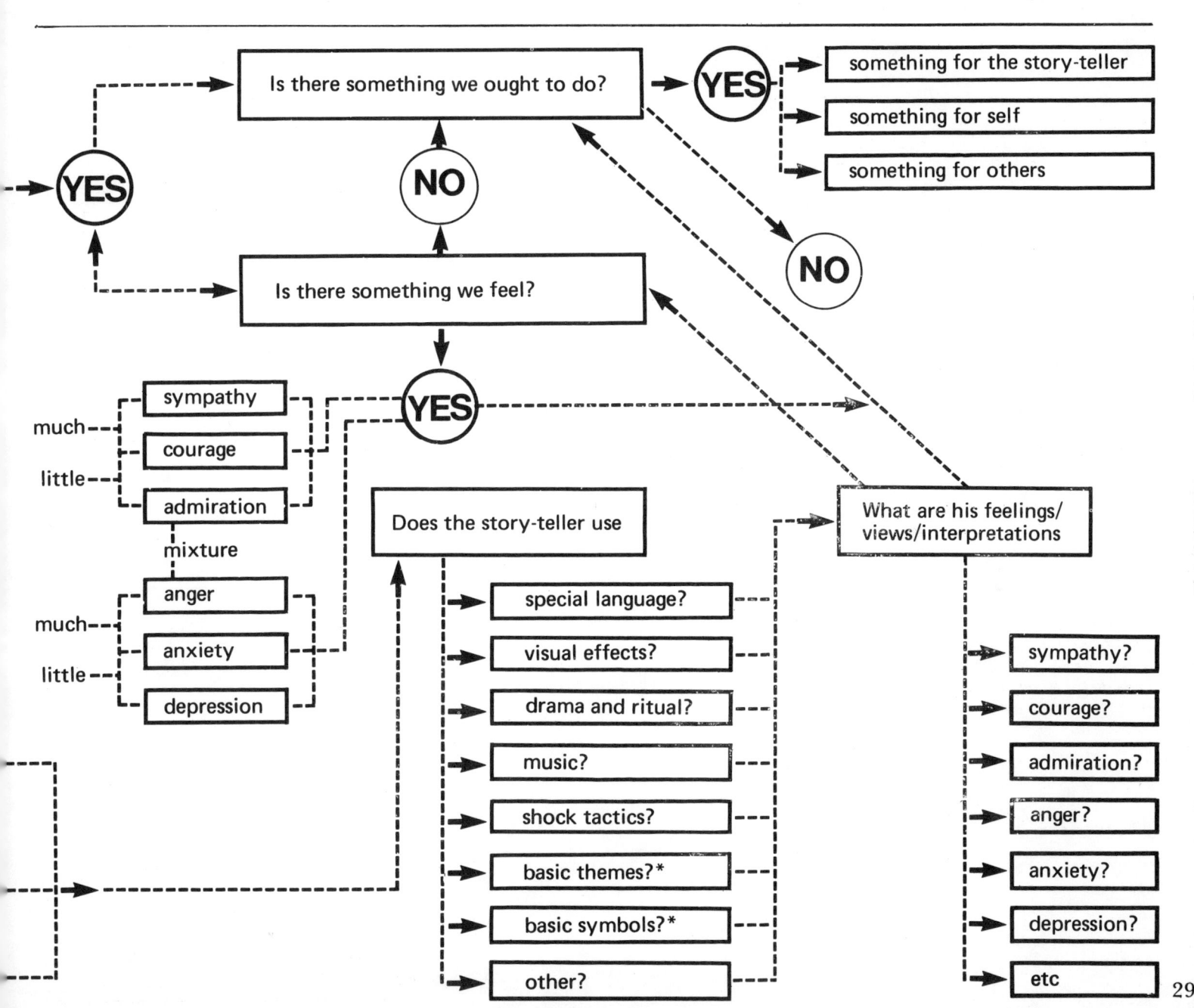

29

 **king**    **queen**    **knight**

MAN

father

mother

sex

sword

mirror

colour

water

fire

blood

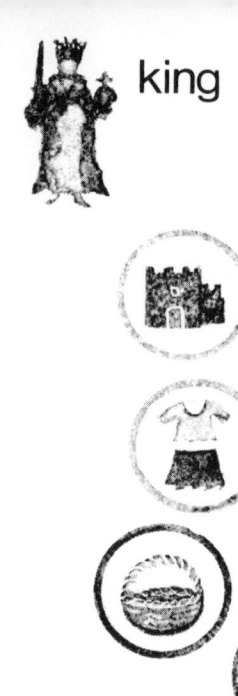

castle / crown

diamonds / crystal

fine clothes

door / basket / key

music

eye

circles / rings / rhythms

banqueting

wine / meat / bread

ropes / chains

weaving

alchemy

dew

running water

mountains

mastery over animals

birds

eggs

seeds

trees

flowers

fish

LIFE

desire for
security
and
pattern

desire for
love
and
friendship

desire to be
creative

desire for
self-respect

sunlight health spring fertility sky day

NATURE

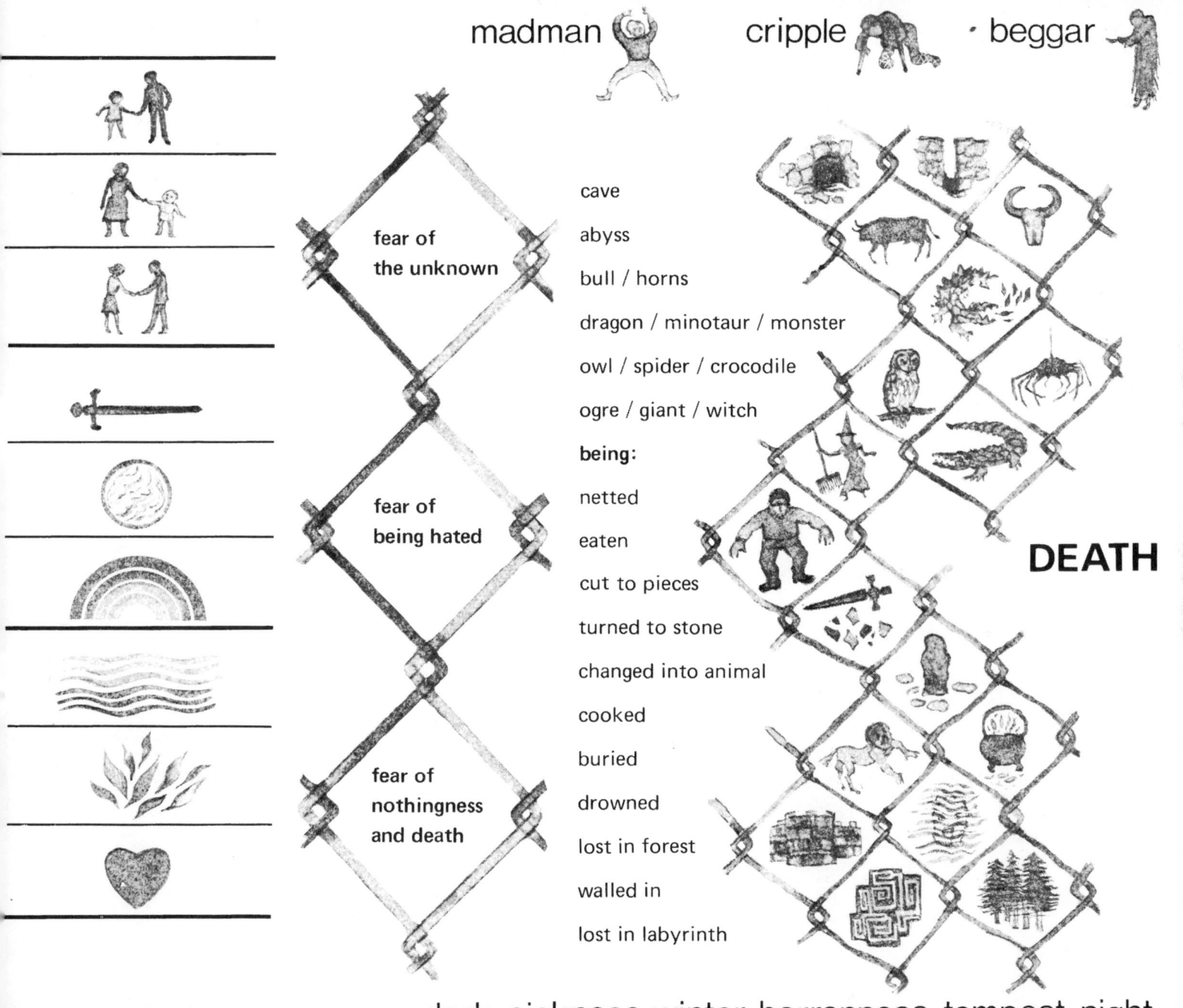

madman   cripple   · beggar

fear of
the unknown

cave

abyss

bull / horns

dragon / minotaur / monster

owl / spider / crocodile

ogre / giant / witch

being:

netted

fear of
being hated

eaten

cut to pieces

turned to stone

changed into animal

cooked

buried

fear of
nothingness
and death

drowned

lost in forest

walled in

lost in labyrinth

DEATH

dark sickness winter barrenness tempest night

symbols

We all of us use symbols all the time, so much so that we do not usually notice them for what they are. We take them for granted. Actually, if we didn't they wouldn't be much good. The point about a symbol is that it expresses a great deal in a very short space of time. Street signs, for example, are symbols: they give the motorist valuable, indeed necessary, information in a very short space of time. The photograph on this page — shows street signs — symbols — at Swiss Cottage, London. *But also the photograph itself is a symbol:* the photographer who took it, who chose to set his camera just there and to click it at just that moment, was trying to express something of what he thought and felt about life in modern cities. Do you agree, that he has expressed a lot in a short space? Do you agree, that he has expressed something in this picture which he could not possibly have expressed so well if he had gone in for intellectual argument? Life is too complicated and too short and too *precious* for us to fritter it away in intellectual arguments. We need symbols. The chart on page 30 shows some of the main symbols, and the themes and experiences with which they are connected, which mankind has ever used — in folktales, mythology, and religon. The chart can be used to explain the impact of (which does *not* mean to 'explain away') some of the stories in this book.

'Facts' and the Journalist

To hear people talking about facts you would think that they lay about like pieces of gold ore in the Yukon days waiting to be picked up — arduously, it is true, but still definitely and visibly — by strenuous prospectors whose subsequent problem was only to get them to market.

Such a view is evidently and dangerously naive. There are no such facts. Or if there are, they are meaningless and totally ineffective; they might, in fact, just as well not be lying about at all until the prospector — or journalist — puts them into relation with other facts; presents them, in other words. Then they become as much a part of a pattern created by him as if he were writing a novel. In that sense all stories are written backwards — they are supposed to begin with the facts and develop from there, but in reality they begin with a journalist's point of view, a conception, and it is the point of view from which the facts are subsequently organised.

Claud Cockburn, England 1960s

'the stilling of the storm'
some relevant points

According to a myth which was widespread in antiquity, and was shared at one time by the Jews, the original act of creation involved God in a desperate, but finally victorious, contest with the forces of chaos and evil, which were identified with, or at any rate located in, the waters of the sea. As a consequence:

(a) ability to control the sea and subdue tempests was regarded as one of the characteristic signs of *divine* power; cf Pss 89, 8–9; 93, 3–4; 106, 8–9; and Isa 51, 9b, 10.

(b) the image of a storm, or of great waters, was frequently used as a metaphor for the evil forces active in the world, and particularly for the tribulations of the righteous, from which only the power of God could save them; cf Ps. 69, 1, 2, 14, 15.

(c) the complete confidence in God the religious man ought always to display can be expressed by saying that even in the most terrible storm he will not doubt God's power and determination to save him; cf Isa 43, 2; Pss 46, 1–3, 65, 5; and on the whole matter see carefully Ps. 107, 23–32.

from 'The Gospel of St Mark' by D E Nineham 1960s

---

a miracle story— *what do you think?*

On that day, when evening came, he said to them, 'Let us go across to the other side.' And leaving the crowd, they took him with them, just as he was, in the boat. And other boats were with him. And a great storm of wind arose, and the waves beat into the boat, so that the boat was already filling. But he was in the stern, asleep on the cushion; and they woke him and said to him, 'Teacher, do you not care if we perish?' And he awoke and rebuked the wind, and said to the sea, 'Peace! Be still!' and the wind ceased, and there was a great calm. He said to them, 'Why are you afraid? Have you no faith?' And they were filled with awe, and said to one another, 'Who then is this, that even wind and sea obey him?'

There are four main possibilities. Which do you think the most likely?

1 There really was a storm. And Jesus really did quell it, quickly and easily, as the story says. i.e. Jesus had power over nature in a way no other man ever has or had.

2 There really was a storm, but what Jesus quelled was the fear and anxiety in the disciples, not the actual waves and wind.

3 There may or may not have been an actual storm. But the disciples *were* anxious about something (other than, or in addition to, the storm), and Jesus did relieve their anxiety.

4 There was neither storm or anxiety. The story grew up without a basis in fact, or was made up deliberately, and was then used to impress people with Jesus' supposed powers.

But would you agree that the *main* question is: what *difference* does believing one or another of these possibilities make?

abandoning the attitude

"*I could understand if today were Sunday . . .*"

Hamm Let us pray to God . . . Off we go.

    (Attitudes of prayer. Silence. Hamm abandons his attitude, discouraged)

Hamm Well?

Clov *(abandoning his attitude)* What a hope! And you?

Hamm Sweet damn all!

Nagg Wait! *(Pause. Abandoning his attitude)* Nothing doing!

Hamm The bastard! He doesn't exist!

from 'Endgame,' by Samuel Beckett, France 1950s

Earth mother we've rolled you on your back, we've ploughed you up, Sky father we're in amongst you, we're carving you up, Siva and Aphrodite you sex-maniacs, we've got you two sorted out, don't come it, we know all about you, Odin we can fight our own battles thank you, and Domovoi lad, you're in the waste-disposal unit, and that's where you belong.

Gods and Goddesses answers to the questions on pages 24—27

Picture 1: ISIS, Egyptian goddess, description (c)
Picture 2: DOMOVOI, Central European god, description (b)

Ladies and Gentlemen, it was great knowing you — really, you were fabulous — but we've had to get rid of you, for various reasons you've had to go, for various reasons you're redundant and an embarrassment, so no hard feelings

A Christian missionary answers questions

An old man said he had a question. 'Which is this god of yours, he asked,' the goddess of the earth, the god of the sky, Amadiora of the thunderbolt, or what?'

The interpreter spoke to the white man and he immediately gave his answer. 'All the gods you have named are not gods at all. They are gods of deceit who tell you to kill your fellows and destroy innocent children. There is only one true God and He has the earth, the sky, you and me and all of us.'

'If we leave our gods and follow your god', asked another man, 'who will protect us from the anger of our neglected gods and ancestors?'

'Your gods are not alive and cannot do you any harm' replied the white man. 'They are pieces of wood and stone.'

When this was interpreted to the men at Mbanta they broke into derisive laughter. These men must be mad, they said to themselves. How else could they say that Ani and Amadoira were harmless? And Idemili and Ogwugwu too? And some of them began to go away.

from 'Things Fall Apart' by Chinva Achebe, Nigeria 1950s
(the setting is Nigeria, at the turn of the century)

Our father which art in heaven,
Stay there.

Anon

Northern Ireland 1970

"It's enough to make you pray for an agnostic revival."

gods, just good-bye, good-bye and man bless you.

Picture 3: SIVA, Indian god, description (a)
Picture 4: ODIN, Northern European god, description (f)

There are three main reasons why we've had to get rid of you. If you're interested, read on now because here — on the next dozen pages of this book — the reasons are.

Picture 5: TEZCATLICOPA, Mexican god, description (e)
Picture 6: APHRODITE, Greek goddess, description (d)

real and really

The Explorers

Once upon a time two explorers came upon a clearing in the jungle. In the clearing were growing many flowers and many weeds. One explorer says, 'Some gardener must tend this plot.' The other disagrees. 'There is no gardener.' So they pitch their tents and set a watch. No gardener is ever seen. 'But perhaps he is an invisible gardener.' So they set up a barbed wire fence. They electrify it. They patrol it with bloodhounds. But no shrieks ever suggest that some intruder has received a shock. No movement of the wire ever betrays an invisible climber. The bloodhounds never give cry. Yet still the Believer is unconvinced. 'But there is a gardener, invisible, intangible, insensible to electric shocks, a gardener who has no scent and makes no sound, a gardener who comes secretly to look after the garden which he loves.' At last the Sceptic despairs. 'But what is left of your original assertion? Just how does what you call an invisible, intangible, eternally elusive gardener differ from an imaginary gardener, or even from no gardener at all?'

from 'New Essays in Philosophical Theology'
by A G N Flew, England 1950s

First, gods, you're crummy.
All right, there are things we can't do.
All right, we admit it,
There are things. We can't for example
Control our armaments, but we're coming on,
And what we're coming on with, gods,
What's helped us sort you and everything out, gods,
Is our minds.

What our minds tell us is:
We have more efficient ways of making
Safety Growth Health Love Kids HAPPINESS
Than you have.
What our minds tell us is
We have neater ways of talking about
Safety Growth Health Love Kids HAPPINESS
Than you have.

I have steadily endeavoured to keep my mind free so as to give up any hypothesis, however much beloved (and I cannot resist forming one on every subject), as soon as facts are shown to be opposed to it.

Charles Darwin, England, nineteenth century

We're not saying you
don't exist, gods,
Whether you exist or not
isn't terribly interesting,
What we're simply saying is
you're not necessary.
What we're simply saying is
There's nothing you can do
Which we can't do
Better.

telling the children

At the age of five or six children are able to use the words *real* and *really*. They are persistent in the questions they ask. What line would you recommend that parents should take when they get asked:

1 Is Robin Hood real?
2 Can animals really talk?
3 Are angels real?
4 Does Father Christmas really bring the presents?
5 Was I really once inside mummy's tummy?
6 Do people really go to heaven when they die?
7 Is the world really round?
8 Did God really make the world?
9 Are ghosts real?
10 Was Jesus really born in a stable?

Some of the possible lines of approach, more or less, are:

'Yes — I'll explain, shall I?'
'Yes — but it's not important, let's talk about something else.'
'Yes — but you'll understand better when you're older.'
'I don't know⎱ ⎰but people used to think so in the olden days.'
'No ⎰ ⎱but some people think so.'
'No — I'll explain, shall I?'

Any way, does it *matter* what children get told about things like these?

The pictures on these pages are of 'God' and were drawn by children in Birmingham, 1960s

have to hate Him

He was ten

He was ten years of age and had hydrocephalus due to an inoperable tumour the size of a very small pea, just at the right place to stop his cerebrospinal fluid from getting out of his head, which is to say that he had water on the brain, that was bursting his head, so that the brain was becoming stretched out into a thinning rim, and his skull bones likewise. He was in excruciating and unremitting pain.

One of my jobs was to put a needle into this ever-increasing fluid to let it out. I had to do this twice a day, and the so-clear fluid that was killing him would leap out at me from his massive ten-year-old head, rising in a brief column to several feet, sometimes hitting my face.

Cases like this are usually less distressing than they might be, because they are often heavily doped, they partially lose their faculties, sometimes an operation helps. He had had several, but the new canal that was made didn't work.

The condition can sometimes be stabilized at the level of being a chronic vegetable for indefinite years — so that the person finally does not seem to suffer. (Do not despair, the soul dies even before the body.)

But this little boy unmistakably endured agony. He would quietly cry in pain. If he would only have shrieked or complained . . . And he knew he was going to die.

He had started reading *The Pickwick Papers.* The one thing he asked God for, he told me, was that he be allowed to finish this book before he died.

He died before it was half-finished.

**from 'The Bird of Paradise' by R D Laing,
England 1960s**

I cannot imagine any omnipotent sentient being sufficiently cruel to create the world we inhabit.

**a character in 'A Severed Head' by Iris Murdoch,
England 1960s**

If the world which we inhabit has been produced in accordance with a Plan we shall have to reckon Nero a saint in comparison with the Author of that plan. Fortunately, however, the evidence of divine purpose is non-existent. We are, therefore, spared the necessity for that attitude of impotent hatred which every brave and humane man would otherwise be called upon to adopt towards the Almighty Tyrant.

Bertrand Russell, England, this century

Nancy came into the kitchen sobbing. 'Ruthie says — Ruthie says — '

Ruth followed, flouncing. 'I said God is retarded.' She sneered at Nancy, *Baaby.'*

'Ruth!' Angela said.

'Retarded?' Piet asked. It was an adjective her generation applied to anything uncooperative. *The retarded teacher kept us all after class. This retarded pen won't write. Frankie is a re-tard.*

'Well He is,' Ruth said. 'He lets little babies die and He makes cats eat birds and all that stuff. I don't want to sing in the choir next fall.'

'I'm sure that'll make God shape up,' Piet said.

from 'Couples' by John Updike, America 1968

A mother and her dead child, shot by soldiers, a scene in 'Battleship Potemkin' directed by Sergei Eisenstein, Russia, 1920s

Aberfan

A man-made mountain of lumpy black treacle collapsed into itself last Friday and slid down upon the school at Aberfan "just after morning prayers." The phrase is not, as I had at first assumed, a distasteful journalistic device for somehow mixing inappropriate irony with an even more cruel piety. The phrase was also used in my presence by some of the stricken people of Aberfan, and with just enough frequency to force one to look for the bleak significance that seems to lurk behind the words.

For here, among this hideous litter of squat, white-painted stone chapels, it is not only the insurance companies who refer to an Act of God. And it is surely to be expected that whatever deity is worshipped — or propitiated — in these scarred valleys should be a harsh and pitiless creature. Faith can move mountains, boyo, but it bloody well won't *stop* them. Mothers and fathers queue outside Bethania Welsh Congregational to identify and weep over the soiled bodies of their children. Nothing nor nobody, curse nor prayer, God nor Coal Board, can now assuage the awful grief and anguish of this pitiful place.

Dennis Potter in 'New Society', 27 October 1966

for the last week
ten hours a day, I have burned the dead,
and with every human body that I burn,
I burn away a particle of faith.
I am burning God.
Corpses — a conveyor belt of corpses,
an endless belt. History . . .
If I knew that — *He* was looking on
(*with revulsion*)
I would have — to hate Him.

Riccardo, who has been working in the gas chambers at Auschwitz; from 'The Representative', by Rolf Hochhuth Germany, this century

our own fate

All Religions issue Bibles against Satan, and say the most injurious things about him, but we never hear his side.

Mark Twain

Then again, gods, you stink,

FIRE EXPLOSION LIGHTNING THUNDERBOLT

EARTHQUAKE SUBTERRANEAN FIRE

RIOT CIVIL COMMOTION STRIKES

LABOUR DISTURBANCES MALICIOUS PERSONS

STORM TEMPEST FLOOD

BURGLARY HOUSEBREAKING LARCENY THEFT

your world stinks.

All of us need to understand that God, or Nature, or Chance, or Evolution, or the Course of History, or whatever you like to call it, can't be trusted any more. We simply must take charge of our own fate.

Edmund Leach, The Reith Lectures 1967

And,

whether it's arthritic-fingered you are, gods,

or just plain thick,

we don't know,

whether it's immature you are or actually vicious,

we don't care,

"Sometimes, you know, I wonder whether we might be spoiling him with these constant sacrifices . . ."

If God did not exist it would be necessary to invent Him.

Voltaire, France, eighteenth century

The various modes of worship which prevailed in the Roman world were all considered by the people as equally true; by the philosopher as equally false; and by the magistrate as equally useful.

Edward Gibbon, England, eighteenth century

The British churchgoer prefers a severe preacher because he thinks a few home truths will do his neighbours no harm.

Bernard Shaw

Religion . . . invents virtues which are sterile and cruel, and invents sins which are no sins at all.

Edmund Gosse, England, nineteenth century

An honest magistrate has lean clerks; a powerful god has fat priests.

Chinese proverb

for what we know is there are jobs to do,

what we care about is there are jobs to do,

mending and improving and healing jobs,

and all you ever do, gods, is either

get in the way, or

make things worse.

atheism

On pages 36—47 the various items relate to three main features of modern atheism. (1) 'The idea of God is scientifically unnecessary.' (2) 'If he exists God cannot, in view of the sufferings of the world, be good.' (3) 'Belief in God generally does much harm, enslaving and corrupting people, and preventing them from reaching their true selves.' You may care to link each picture or quotation on pages 36—47 to one or another of these ideas.

"It might have been all right two thousand years ago, but I doubt if it's the right image for a modern curate!"

CHIC

'get to know the place'

Wouldn't we all do better not trying to understand, accepting the fact that no human being will ever understand another, not a wife a husband, a lover a mistress, nor a parent a child? Perhaps that's why men have invented God — a being capable of understanding. Perhaps if I wanted to be understood or to understand I would bamboozle myself into belief, but I am a reporter; God exists only for leader-writers.

from 'The Quiet American' by Graham Greene, England, this century

This quotation was shown to some young sixthformers. Here are some of the things they said, by way of reaction. Which is closest to your own reaction?

a) 'Surely it would be incredibly boring if we stopped trying to understand each other? We would become even more self-centred. And, Mr Reporter, you seem to be a very naive fellow, not even interested in analysing yourself to find your faults, just interested in reporting "facts" and scandals for your magazine or newspaper.'

b) 'The writer believes that religion is an emotional prop for mentally unbalanced or worried people. A person with a healthy mind has no need of God, according to this man. My reaction is *complete* agreement. An excellent interpretation of why man has invented God.'

c) 'Well I am young, but I believe two people can get to understand one another. We all understand each other to a greater or lesser degree. This to me is very much the whole process of living — to get to understand one another. We won't understand all, but we are always making new discoveries. This man seems to have given up hope.'

d) 'I feel that this writer is incapable of understanding or being understood himself for he seems to be talking nonsense. Maybe it is myself that is incapable of understanding. But I feel that it is much easier to understand a fellow human being whom we can see, touch, and be aware of, than to understand God whom we are not even sure exists.'

e) 'This is a man who won't look honestly at what Christianity is saying.'

'Glorying in the cross': a scene in
'The Dance of the Seven Veils'
directed by Ken Russell, England, 1960s

New Approach Needed

Should you revisit us,
Stay a little longer,
And get to know the place.
Experience hunger,
Madness, disease and war.
You heard about them, true,
The last time you came here;
It's different having them.
And what about a go
At sex, marriage, children?
All good, but bringing some
Risk of remorse and pain
And fear of an odd sort:
A sort one should, again,
Feel, not just hear about,
To be qualified as
A human-race expert.
On local life, we trust
The resident witness,
Not the royal tourist.

People have suffered worse
And more durable wrongs
Than you did on that cross
(I know — you won't get me
Up on one of those things)
Without much prospect of
Ascending good as new
On the third day, without
'I die, but man shall live'
As a nice cheering thought.

So, next time, come off it,
And get some service in,
Jack, long before you start
To lay down the old law:
If you still want to then,
Tell your dad that from me.

Kingsley Amis, England 1960s

Third, gods,
you never grew up, you never got beyond the infant stage,
and because of this, because of this, gods,
because even though you call yourselves mother and father
you are really a pack of pathetic weak kids,
because of this, you try to cover up, try to cover your insecurity,
and try to keep us in, try to push us around,
try to pin us down, try to make us pathetic kids too.

Well we are not having any, well.

We are bigger men, gods,
Than you ever were.
Well.

that obedient flock

Circumscripture

As Pastor X steps out of bed
  he slips a neat disguise on:
that halo round his priestly head
  is really his horizon.

Piet Hein, Denmark, this century

"It's an emissary of the Church."

(At the time of the Spanish Inquisition Christ has come back to earth; he has been arrested and thrown into prison; he is visited by the Grand Inquisitor on the eve of his execution; the Inquisitor says:)

'Come down from the cross' men said, 'and we will believe that you are the messiah'. But you would not come down, for you refused to enslave men with miracles. You asked for love given freely, not for the base raptures of a slave. But in this you were thinking too highly of men. I swear to you, man is weaker and viler in his nature than you believed him to be. Can he, can he do what you did? By showing him so much respect, you ceased to feel for him, for you asked too much of him, far too much. Respecting him less you would have asked less of him. That would have been more like love, for his burden would have been lighter. He is weak and vile.

  But we, we in the Church, have corrected your work, and we have founded it upon miracle and authority. Men rejoice that they are again led like sheep, and that the terrible gift which you brought has at last been lifted from their hearts. And tomorrow you will see that obedient flock who at a sign from me will hasten to heap up the hot cinders about the pile on which I shall burn you for coming to hinder us. For if anyone, ever deserved our fires it was you. Tomorrow I shall burn you.

from 'The Brothers Karamazov' by Fydor Dostoievsky Russia, nineteenth century

Now, if the gods could speak now what would they say now? Now, if the gods in fact had power now what would they do now? What would they say and do to us as we leave them behind, what would they say and do to us as we sever all relations with them? Swear, rage, roar, shriek, stamp, chuck thunderbolts? The worst of them surely would, but what we want to know is what the best of them would say, the best gods, what we want to know is what the best of them would give us to help us on our way, what we want to know is what pictures the best of them would suggest. What pictures? What pictures? The best? The best?

Above: 'Better to reign in hell than to serve in heaven':
Lucifer seeks to arouse rebel angels. Water-colour
by William Blake, England, nineteenth century.

Right: 'Faith' — from a picture by Pieter Bruegel,
Holland, sixteenth century.

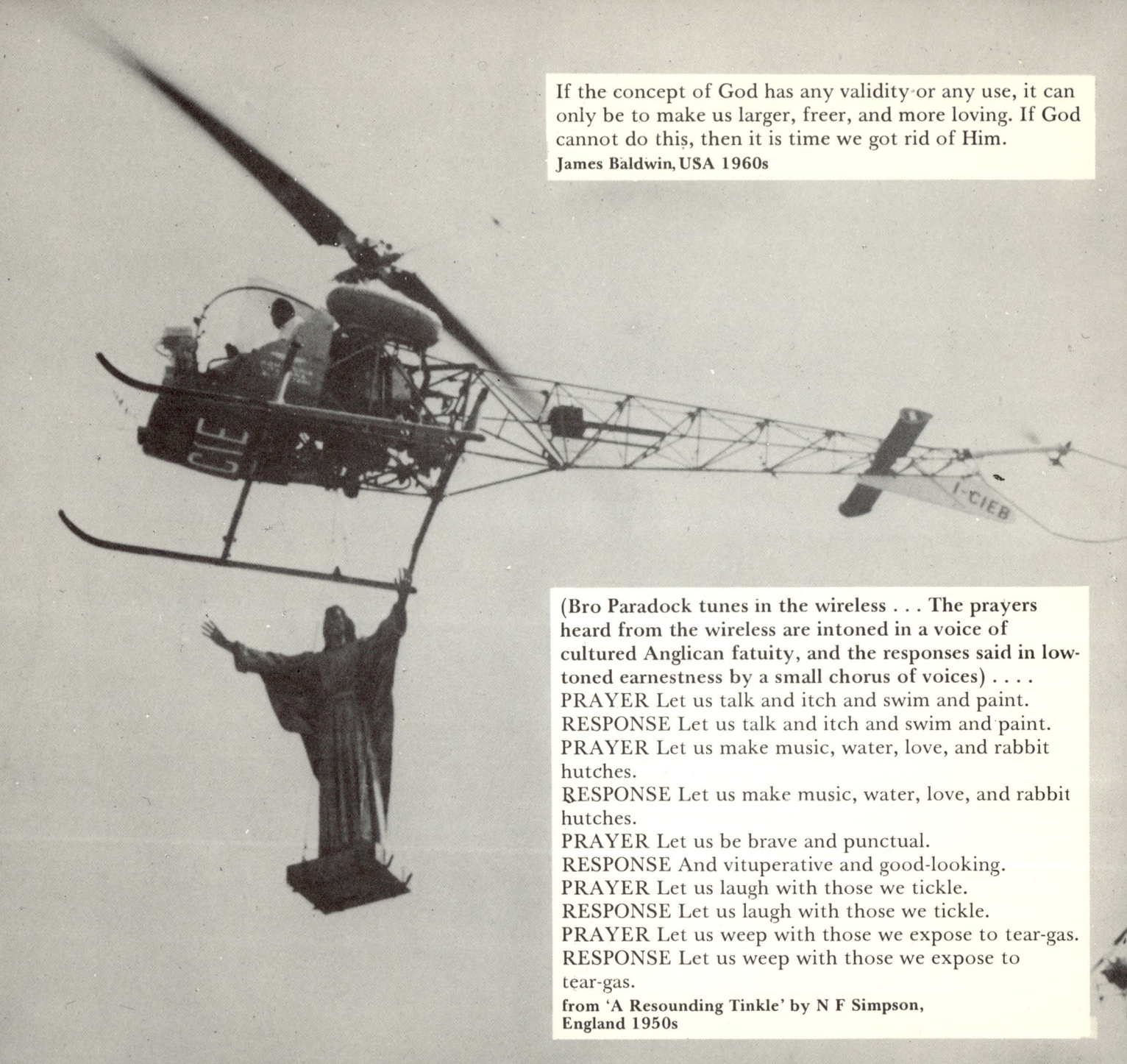

If the concept of God has any validity or any use, it can only be to make us larger, freer, and more loving. If God cannot do this, then it is time we got rid of Him.
James Baldwin, USA 1960s

(Bro Paradock tunes in the wireless . . . The prayers heard from the wireless are intoned in a voice of cultured Anglican fatuity, and the responses said in low-toned earnestness by a small chorus of voices) . . . .
PRAYER Let us talk and itch and swim and paint.
RESPONSE Let us talk and itch and swim and paint.
PRAYER Let us make music, water, love, and rabbit hutches.
RESPONSE Let us make music, water, love, and rabbit hutches.
PRAYER Let us be brave and punctual.
RESPONSE And vituperative and good-looking.
PRAYER Let us laugh with those we tickle.
RESPONSE Let us laugh with those we tickle.
PRAYER Let us weep with those we expose to tear-gas.
RESPONSE Let us weep with those we expose to tear-gas.
from 'A Resounding Tinkle' by N F Simpson, England 1950s

The Weak Monk

The monk sat in his den
He took the mighty pen
And wrote: 'Of God and Men'.

One day the thought struck him
It was not according to Catholic doctrine,
His blood ran dim.

He wrote till he was ninety years old
Then he shut the book with a clasp of gold
And buried it under the sheepfold.

He'd enjoyed it so much, he loved to plod,
And he thought he'd a right to expect that God
Would rescue his book alive from the sod.

Of course it rotted in the snow and rain,
No one will ever know now what he wrote of God and
Men.

For this the monk is to blame.

Stevie Smith, England 1960s

**Left: a scene in the film 'La Dolce Vita',
directed by Frederico Fellini, Italy 1960s**

"*They're not coming in like they used to. We'll have to start raising
the ban on agnostics.*"

From now on the pages of this book are pictures of, and from now on the pages of this book are pictures for, a
journey . . . . a journey from and a journey to.

what he really meant

Germany, fifteenth century

Italy, fourteenth century

Some people would not mind knowing what he really meant: self, neighbour, god, which latter (it is said) he spelt God. But self, love thyself, would that mean: dance because you are you, with these hands (this hump of a nail, this skin, these veins, smudges, these happy knuckles) and with this head your busy nerve-centre, and twirl and dance for

48

From a painting by John Bratby, England, 1960s

your sex, and leap, caper for the channels, wires, waves in your body, for all that draws you together, all, all, leave nothing out, leave no stone unturned, prance to a mirror and look with more than your eyes at more than your eyes, and yell: Marvellous!

Self, love thyself, would that also mean: get out and at em, get out and about, get weaving, a move on, stuck in, let the old world know you exist, smashing a bit here maybe and whittling a bit there, leaving a dent or a thumbprint, but mainly building a whole lot all over the place, making the world a different place, that's all, making sure there are silences and gaps entered which would not have been if you had not passed by and entered them, that's all, and fingering, contemplating, remembering what you have built, achieved, and thinking: marvellous! That's all.

the side of progress

Neighbour, love thy neighbour, would that mean: grin all over your face that he's there, grin, caper, prance, that your friend has arms, legs, neck, waist, sex, that your wife, lover, boyfriend, girlfriend, has lashes, freckles, lips, wisps of hair, that your mistress, workmate, colleague, helper, next desk, next seat, next bench, is *there*, also your mum, dad, gran, kids, your boss, leader, king, your employee, also your worst enemy, would it mean all them.

Love

Love bade me welcome: yet my soul drew back,
    Guiltie of dust and sinne.
But quick-ey'd Love, observing me grow slack
    From my first entrance in,
Drew nearer to me, sweetly reasoning,
    If I lacked anything.

A guest, I answer'd, worthy to be here:
    Love said, You shall be he.
I the unkinde, ungratefull? Ah my deare,
    I cannot look on thee.
Love took my hand, and smiling did reply,
    Who made the eyes but I?

Truth Lord, but I have marr'd them: let my shame
    Go where it doth deserve.
And know you not, sayes Love, who bore the blame?
    My deare, then I will serve.
You must sit down, sayes Love, and taste my meat:
    So I did sit and eat.

George Herbert, England, seventeenth century

'. . . and how did it end?'

Neighbour, love thy neighbour, would that also mean: notice in the eyes, the skin, the gesture, the voice, tiredness, fear, depression, impatience, would that also mean in the eyes, the skin, the gesture, the voice, notice pleasure, hope, rejoicing, and would that also mean bothering, and doing something (or not doing something, as the case may be) in order that he can, in order that he can, in order that he can: better love himself.

Where there is love there is God **Russian proverb**

a conversation between two atheists
'. . . We have become cynical about progress because of the terrible things we have seen men do during the last forty years. All the same through trial and error the amoeba did become the ape. There were blind starts and wrong turnings even then, I suppose. Evolution today can produce Hitlers as well as St John of the Cross. I have a small hope, that's all, a very small hope, that someone they call Christ was the fertile element, looking for a crack in the wall to plant its seed. I think of Christ as an amoeba who took the right turning. I want to be on the side of the progress which survives. I'm no friend of pterodactyls.'

'But if we are incapable of love?'

'I'm not sure such a man exists. Love is planted in man now, even uselessly in some cases, like an appendix. Sometimes of course people call it hate.'

'I haven't found any trace of it in myself.'

'Perhaps you are looking for something too big and too important. Or too active.'

'What you are saying seems to me every bit as superstitious as what the fathers believe.'

'Who cares? It's the superstition I live by.'

from 'A Burnt Out Case' by Graham Greene, England 1950s. The reference to 'fathers' is to Roman Catholic priests

Kaliayev A time will come when . . . we shall all be brothers, and when we shall all be utterly honest with one another. Do you know what I'm talking about?

Foka Yes, the Kingdom of God.

Kaliayev No, you mustn't say that. There's nothing God can do. Setting things right is our business, not His. (*Pause*) You don't understand? Do you know the story of Saint Dimitri?

Foka No.

Kaliayev He had an appointment in the steppes with God Himself, and he was hurrying there when he met a peasant, whose cart was stuck in the mud. So Saint Dimitri helped him. The mud was thick, and the wheel was deep into it. It took them an hour of struggling to get it out. When they had finished, Saint Dimitri ran for the appointment. But God was not still there.

Foka So?

Kaliayev So there are people who will always arrive late for their appointments with God, because there are too many carts stuck in the mud, there are too many brothers who have got to be helped.

from 'The Just' by Albert Camus, France 1950s. The setting is Russia at the turn of the century

Enemy, love thy enemy, would that mean: always reckoning to state his case as well as he can state it himself, and always hoping he'll see the light, if it is light, for himself, so never pushing him around, and would that mean: never demanding an apology, never making him look or feel small, and never hitting back if the purpose is to relieve your own feelings, and enemy love thy enemy would that maybe mean: actually never hitting back, would that maybe mean: actually letting him kill you.

In a manger laid and wrapp'd I was,
So very poor, this was my chance,
Betwixt an ox and a silly poor ass,
To call my true love to my dance.

medieval carol

'The Deposition' by Jan van Dyck, Holland seventeenth century

of the Crucifixion:
Since this moment the universe is
no longer what it was; nature has
received another meaning; history
is transformed; and you and I are
no more, and should not be any
more, what we were before.

Paul Tillich, USA 1950s

'The Deposition' by Graham Sutherland,
England 1940s

bond of love

This quotation was shown to young sixformers:

Litany for the Ghetto

O God, who hangs on street corners, who tastes the grace of cheap wine and the sting of the needle,

Help us to touch you.

O God, whose name is spick, black-nigger, bastard, guinea and kike,

Help us to know you.

Robert Castle, USA 1960s

Here are some of the things they wrote.
Which is the best interpretation do you think?

a) 'The alcoholic, junky, and rich and poor alike, are equal in the eyes of God, and all have an equal chance of getting to heaven and to see God. God lives not only in and around holy people. Everyone can speak to God, no matter what sort of language he uses.'

b) 'Even God has suffered abuse etc. and we ought to be able to put up with our minor troubles instead of moaning all the time. It shows what God did and put up with for us.'

c) 'To some extent he's blaming God for the evils of the world. Or else he's saying how can there be a God, supposedly benevolent, when there's so much wrong with the world?'

d) 'This is from the quote 'when you do this for the least of mine you do this for me.' It means help the downtrodden! If we call ourselves Christians we should regard every man as a brother — God is everyman we see or meet, people are human beings not animals. Writer is asking for help to be a better Christian.'

I know a man who desired the salvation of his brethren so fervently that he often besought God with burning tears and with his whole heart . . . that either his brethren might be saved with him, or he might be condemned with them. For he was bound to them in the Holy Spirit, by such a bond of love that he did not even wish to enter the kingdom of heaven if to do so meant being separated from them.

St Symeon, Russia, middle ages

God gives the drinker the vine but not the goblet.

German proverb

God is better pleased with adverbs than with nouns.

Old English proverb

Here are quotations from what various people have said about religion. To what extent, if any, would you also say things along the same lines:	not at all	hardly at all	partly	quite a lot	a great deal
1 'Being a Christian does not necessarily involve believing in God and heaven etc.'					
2 'For me, it is belief in God that gives life meaning.'					
3 'It is quite possible that people are born again a certain number of years after their death. (i.e. reincarnation)'					
4 'I am not sure that Jesus even ever existed.'					
5 'I grew up believing the Christian faith to be true, and now tend to accept it for myself'.					
6 'The churches seem more concerned with their own affairs than with major problems such as war, injustice etc.'					
7 'For me, God is like a real person who helps you throughout your life.'					
8 'It's not God we should thank for supplying our everyday needs, but farmers, scientists, technicians etc.'					
9 'One should take the resurrection of Jesus as a symbol. It doesn't matter whether it actually happened or not.'					
10 'I frequently feel strengthened and inspired by the service of Holy Communion.'					
11 'I believe in the resurrection of Jesus, and I therefore believe that I shall survive death also.'					
12 'I tend to be turned against the Christian faith by the fact that many who call themselves Christians do not in fact live a Christian life.'					
13 'Compulsory attendance at school religious services has tended to turn me against the Christian faith.'					
14 'As I see it, those who take the lead to relieve suffering and injustice are mainly people who accept Christian religious beliefs.'					
15 'The personality is different from the physical body, and it is probable that it survives death.'					
16 'I find prayer a source of guidance and strength.'					
17 'The fact that few members of my generation accept the Christian faith has tended to influence me against it also.'					
18 'On the whole it's pointless to spend time wondering what the purpose of life is or might be.'					

what it's all for

Resurrection:
from a painting
by Stanley Spencer,
England 1920s

World Religions — answers to questions on page 49.

1 Hinduism   2 Buddhism   3 Buddhism

4 Hinduism   5 Islam   6 Buddhism   7 The Koran

8 Taoism   9 Buddha   10 Islam

The way to God lies through love of people, and there is no other way.

Sergei Hackel, Russia this century

Imagine yourself as a living house. God comes in to rebuild that house. At first, perhaps, you can understand what He is doing. He is getting the drains right and stopping the leaks in the roof and so on: you knew that these jobs needed doing and so you are not surprised. But presently he starts knocking the house about in a way that hurts abominably and does not seem to make sense. What on earth is He up to? The explanation is that He is building quite a different house from the one you thought of — throwing out a new wing here, putting on an extra floor there, running up towers, making courtyards. You thought you were going to be made into a decent little cottage: but He is building a palace. He intends to come and live in it Himself.

C S Lewis, England 1940s

I thank you, God, for all that you have given me, and for all that You may yet give me, whether good or bad. I bless you for everything You do and for all that You are. I have pity for You, God, and I forgive You Your suffering and Your cruelty in me and in all men. I love You, God, I am yours, I no longer exist; there is only You, the victory is Yours, my victory is Yours because I give it to You with all my heart, because Your victory is in my heart. Blessed be God, my love, my happiness, my grief, love of the universe, grief of the universe, be blessed, my God, my God, God

the end of 'Incognito' by Petru Dumitriu, Rumania 1950s

'Would you like to call Heaven tonight? You can reverse the charges you know. Oh, yes, brother, reverse the charges.' He swung from his audience, a girl with a jump rope and a Chinese laundryman pausing in the gutter with his pushcart to eat a candy bar, toward us as we approached. 'Oh yes brother, reverse the charges. *He'll* accept them. He's paid for your call with the ultimate price — His Son Jesus Christ! It's all paid for, all on the house, all for free! Just pick up the phone and tell the operator — that's the Holy Ghost, you know — 'Get me Heaven, please. Put me through to God Almighty.'

from 'The Blood of the Lamb' by Peter de Vries, USA 1960s

God, love thy God, would that mean: FREAK amino acids synthesise in electric storm FREAK amino acids join forces to be proteins FREAK DNA and RNA thrown up also FREAK proteins and DNA stage a happy union FREAK plant life in sea FREAK plant life on land FREAK worms jellyfish trilobites sea-scorpions sharks millipedes salamanders ichthyosaurus dinosaurs sea-cows elephants gibbons FREAK proconsuls pliopithecus australopithecus FREAK neanderthal FREAK homo sapiens FREAK FREAK hunting harvesting herding laws cities FREAK Jesus Christ love thy neighbour love love love NOT A FREAK THIS IS WHAT'S IT'S ALL FOR THIS IS WHAT IT'S ALL ABOUT AND EVEN IF IT ISN'T LIVE AS IF IT IS YOU'VE GOT THE WHOLE WORLD IN YOUR HANDS REPEAT NOT A FREAK REPEAT EVEN IF IT IS A FREAK LIVE AS IF IT'S ALL FOR LOVE E.G. SUPREMELY JESUS CHRIST.

where there is nothing

Rest in the position of doing nothing, and things will take care of themselves. Relax your body, spit out your intelligence, forget about principles and things. Cast yourself into the ocean of existence, unshackle your mind, free your spirit, make yourself as quiet as an inanimate being.

Chuang Tzu, China, 5th century BC

To look for reality by means of the senses is like searching for the son of a barren woman, or feeling for the horns of a hare, or looking for a bird's footprint in the sky.

Indian saying

If a man sleeps in a damp place, he will wake up with an aching back, and feeling half dead; but is this true of an eel? If men tried to live in trees they would be scared out of their wits; but are monkeys? Of the three, which knows the right place to live? Men eat meat; deer eat grass; centipedes like snakes; owls and crows enjoy mice. Will you tell me please which of these four has the correct taste?

Chuang Tzu

A certain man came to the Buddha and said: 'I want to know whether there is a life after death, I want to know whether man has a soul, I want to know is the world eternal, and if you do not give me satisfactory answers I shall not be your follower.' The Buddha replied:

'It is as if a man had been wounded by an arrow
   thickly smeared with poison,
and his friends, companions, relatives and kinsmen
   were to fetch a surgeon to heal him
and he were to say:

"I will not have this arrow pulled out
   until I know by what man I was wounded
whether he is of the warrior caste, or a brahmin,
or of the lowest caste.

"And

"I will not have this arrow pulled out
   until I know whether the bow with which I was
wounded
was a chapa or a konanda,
or until I know whether the bow-string was of
swallow-wort
or bamboo-fibre, or sinew, or hemp, or of milk-sap tree,
or until I know whether the shaft was from
a wild or cultivated plant,
or whether it was feathered from a vulture's wing
or a heron's or a hawk's or a peacock's
or a sithilahanu-bird's."

That man would surely die.'

Buddhist scriptures

We put thirty spokes together and call it a wheel;
But it is on the space where there is nothing that
   the usefulness of the wheel depends.
We turn clay to make a vessel;
But it is on the space where there is nothing that
   the usefulness of the vessel depends.
We pierce doors and windows to make a house;
And it is on these spaces where there is nothing
   that the usefulness of the house depends.
Therefore just as we take advantage of what is,
   we should recognise the usefulness of what is
   not.

Lao Tzu, translated Arthur Waley, China, fifth century BC

When you've seen beyond yourself —
Then you may find peace of mind is
waiting there.
And the time will come when you see
we're all one, and life flows on within
you and without you.

Song, England 1960s

India, first centuries A D

life generous

some questions and answers in Zen Buddhism

question   *Everybody has a place of birth. What is your place of birth?*
answer   Early this morning I ate white rice gruel. Now I'm hungry again.

question   *How is my hand like the Buddha's hand?*
answer   Playing the lute under the moon.

question   *How is my foot like a donkey's foot?*
answer   When the white heron stands in the snow it has a different colour.

India, first centuries A D

on Taoism, and the idea of 'te'

... te is the unthinkable ingenuity and creative power of man's spontaneous and natural functioning — a power which is blocked when one tries to master it in terms of formal methods and techniques. It is like the centipede's skill in using a hundred legs at once:

A centipede was happy, quite,
Until a toad in fun
Said, 'Pray, which leg goes after which?'
This worked his mind to such a pitch,
He lay distracted in a ditch,
Considering how to run.

A profound regard for te underlies the entire higher culture of the Far East, so much so that it has been made the basic principle of every kind of art and craft ...

from 'The Way of Zen' by Alan Watts, USA 1950s

meditation

On page 58 there is some advice from Chuang Tzu, the ancient Chinese writer, on meditation. You may care to try it. Here are some further suggestions:

1 Sit in a relaxed but active position: on a straightbacked chair, maybe, hands resting lightly on thighs.
2 Either close your eyes or else gaze on some particular object — a flower, a vase, a stone, a lighted candle — placed in front of you.
3 Notice your own breathing, and feel it, so to speak; and notice your body, become aware of your limbs, your fingertips.
4 When irrelevant thoughts come into your mind (which they will) don't eject them with force; but don't welcome them either; take no notice of them; just let them float around, and watch them mildly; they'll soon leave.
5 Imagine a blank screen in your mind's eye; let pictures appear on it — maybe of a person whom you know, a memory from the past, a plan for the future; watch the pictures carefully, but with detachment; try to understand — but without grabbing, striving — what is going on.
6 As you return to the everyday world, wonder what the consequences are going to be, if any.

God, love God, would that mean also: love yourself for your self and your self for your neighbour, THOUGH SINCE: you cannot, THOUGH SINCE: you are only human, THOUGH SINCE: your mother's milk was a mixture and your father's hands were softandhard, THOUGH SINCE: both your employer/teacher and your employee/pupil can drain/freeze you, THOUGH SINCE: your friends' eyes can scratch you and the sex of your man/woman can stab/swallow you, THOUGH SINCE, THOUGH SINCE (repeat): youcannotwhollylovebecauseyouarenotwhollylovedbecauseyouareonlyhuman . . . . know yourself loved by, know yourself trusted by, life . . . . know that life sings and kisses you to love your self . . . . . know that life generous is like generous your generous father/your mother/your bride/your bridegroom generous LIFE.HAS NO SENSE OF THE VALUE OF MONEY LIFE SPENT A BIT OF ITSELF FOR YOU HOW FANTASTIC HOW MARVELLOUS YOU CAN LOVE AND TRUST LIFE IN RETURN HOW ABOUT THAT.

unknown

God speaks to man

Brace yourself and stand up like a man;
I will ask questions, and you shall answer.
Where were you when I laid the earth's foundations?
Tell me, if you know and understand.
Who settled its dimensions? Surely you should know.
Who stretched his measuring line over it?
On what do its supporting pillars rest?
Who set its corner-stone in place,
when the morning stars sang together
and all the sons of God shouted aloud?
Who watched over the birth of the sea,
when it burst in flood over the womb? —
when I wrapped it in a blanket of cloud
and cradled it in fog,
when I established its bounds,
fixing its doors and bars in place,
and said, 'Thus far shall you come and no further,
and here your surging waves shall halt.'
In all your life have you ever called up the dawn
or shown the morning its place?

The book of Job, Hebrew 500 BC

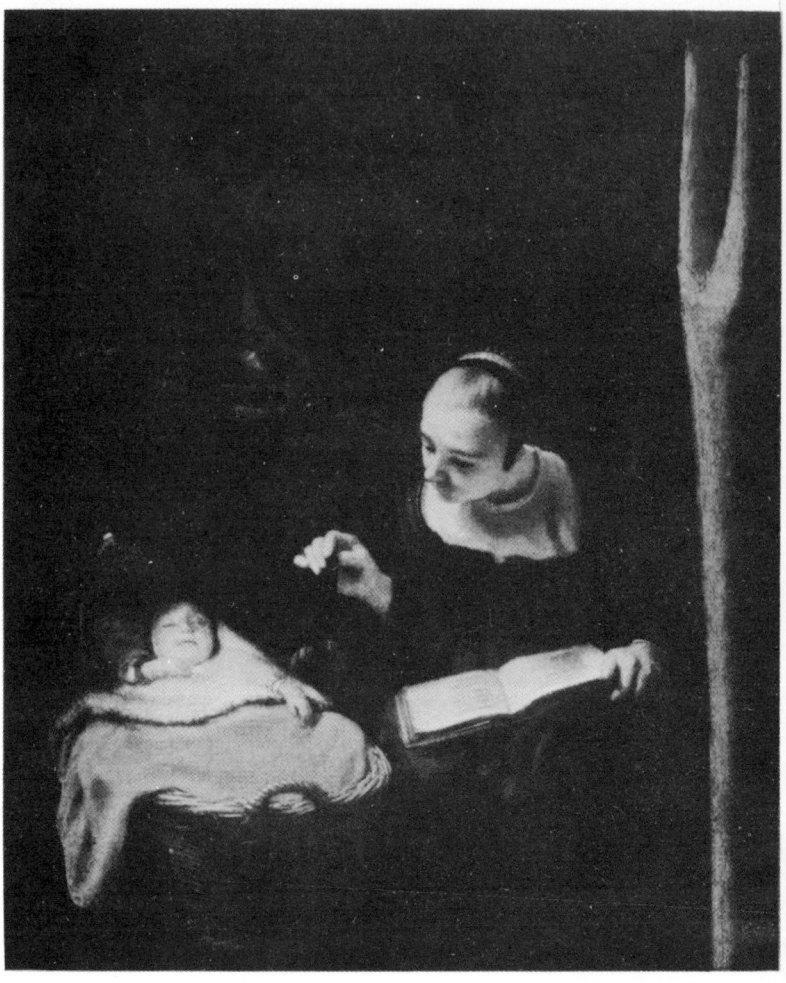

God, love God, would that also mean: love the unknown. God, love God, would that also mean: turn and look with eyes wide at the unknown just (just, just) over your shoulder, the unknown. Would it mean: never mind about the unknown, *it's all right*, never mind about not knowing, *it's all right*, and let the stars the witches the ghosts the gods the gods also the gods drop drop drop the names of them drop but love the mystery, the mystery, love the mystery which begins, which stretches, on both sides of your skin. God, love God, would that mean TRUSTING LIFTING

THE FACE TO WAITING FOR EMBRACING THE UNKNOWN

I suddenly felt as if some ancient mist had in a moment lifted from my sight, and the ultimate significance of all things was laid bare . . . I found what had been detached and dim had a great unity of meaning, as if a man groping through a fog suddenly discovers that he stands before his own house . . . An unexpected train of thought ran across my mind like a strange caravan carrying the wealth of an unknown kingdom . . . Immediately I found the world bathed in a wonderful radiance with waves of beauty and joy swelling on every side, and no person or thing in the world seemed to me trivial or unpleasing.

Rabindranath Tagore, India this century

God changes his appearance every second. Blessed is the man who can recognise him in all his disguises. At one moment he is a glass of fresh water, the next your son bouncing on your knees or an enchanting woman, or perhaps merely a morning walk.

Little by little, everything around me, without changing shape, became a dream. I was happy. Earth and paradise were one. A flower in the fields with a large drop of honey in its centre: that was how life appeared to me. And my soul, a wild bee plundering.

from 'Zorba the Greek' by Nikos Kazantzakis, Crete, this century

Left: 'Life may be trusted': mother and child by Nicholaes Maes, Holland, seventeenth century

Mother and Child by Henry Moore, England 1920s

Remember oh remember the gods can HOW (it is their speciality) rise from the dead WHEN and some WHICH can bind us, age us, can suck our blood WHY and some WHICH can make things, oh all things, new, new, WHETHER new, can make all things, oh, all, all things WHOSE new.

acknowledgements

Acknowledgement is made to the following for permission to reproduce copyright material:

Illustrations

Victoria and Albert Museum, 2, 25, 45, 48
Pitt Rivers Museum, Oxford, 3
Punch, 4, 9, 10, 18, 20, 34, 35, 40, 41, 44
Bayerische Staatsbibliothek Munich, 7
Universal Pictures, 11
Connoisseur Films, 13
Ashmolean Museum, Oxford, 14, 52, 59, 60
Svensk Filmindustrie, 16
Bodleian Library, Oxford, 22
Cyril Bernard, 23
Musée du Louvre, Paris, 24
Bilibine, and Larousse Encyclopaedia of Mythology, 25, 27
Ny Carsberg Glyptothek, Copenhagen, 26
Tate Gallery, London, 27, 56
Council of Industrial Design, 32
The Birmingham Post and Mail Ltd, 36, 37
Peter Boyce, 37
Contemporary Films, 38
BBC, 42, 43
Piet Hein, and Hodder and Stoughton Ltd, 44
Museum Boymans-van Beuningen, Rotterdam, 45
Rizzoli Film Company, 46
St. Martin's College, Lancaster, 49
Papas and *The Guardian,* 50
Fitzwilliam Museum, Cambridge, 53
Rijksmuseum, Amsterdam, 62
Manchester City Art Galleries, 63

Poems

Heather Ryan, and the Daily Mirror Children's Literary Competition, page 10; Erich Fried for the poem 'Definition' on page 14, translated by Georg Rapp, from *On Pain of Seeing,* published by Rapp and Whiting; Kingsley Amis and Jonathan Cape Ltd for 'New Approach Needed', from *A Look Round the Estate,* 43; Stevie Smith and Longmans, Green and Co. Ltd. for 'The Weak Monk' from *Selected Poems* (also in *Penguin Modern Poets 8*), 47.

References

In addition to references given in the text, books referred to or quoted from are:
Lore and Language of Schoolchildren by Peter and Iona Opie, pages 2, 3; *The Unknown Gods of the English* by David Martin, printed in *The Listener* and in *The Religious and the Secular,* 5; *The Listener* 1967, 16; *Learning for Living* 17; *Good Housekeeping,* 17; *Look, Stay and Enjoy* by Robin Richardson, 19; *Oxford Dictionary,* 22; *I Claud* by Claud Cockburn, 32; *The Fire Next Time* by James Baldwin, 46; *Within You and Without You* by George Harrison, 59.